THE PALM VALLEY SCHOOL

For Excellence In
Poetry Recitation
1997 - 1998
Grade 3
Emily Smith

A·BOOK·OF·VERSES·
FOR·CHILDREN·

SMITHMARK

First published 1897 by Chatto & Windus

This edition published in 1996 by SMITHMARK Publishers,
a division of U.S. Media Holdings, Inc.,
16 East 32nd Street, New York, NY 10016.

SMITHMARK books are available for bulk purchase
for sales promotion and premium use.
For details write or call the manager of special sales,
SMITHMARK Publishers, 16 East 32nd Street,
New York, NY 10016; (212) 532-6600.

Produced by Leopard, a division of Random House UK Ltd,
20 Vauxhall Bridge Road, London SW1V 2SA, UK

ISBN 0-7651-9654-9

Printed and bound in Great Britain

10 9 8 7 6 5 4 3 2 1

PREFACE

You must understand that there is a kind of poetry that is finer far than anything here : poetry to which this book is, in the old-fashioned phrase, simply a " stepping-stone." When you feel, as I hope some day you will feel, that these pages no longer satisfy, then you must turn to the better thing.

E. V. L.

INDEX

TWO THOUGHTS

Happy Thought ✧ ✧

THE world is so full of a number of things,
I'm sure we should all be as happy as kings.
Robert Louis Stevenson.

The World's Music ✧ ✧

THE world's a very happy place,
Where every child should dance and sing,
And always have a smiling face,
And never sulk for anything.

I waken when the morning's come,
And feel the air and light alive
With strange sweet music like the hum
Of bees about their busy hive.

The linnets play among the leaves
At hide-and-seek, and chirp and sing;
While, flashing to and from the eaves, .
The swallows twitter on the wing.

The twigs that shake, and boughs that sway ;
  And tall old trees you could not climb ;
And winds that come, but cannot stay,
  Are gaily singing all the time.

From dawn to dark the old mill-wheel
  Makes music, going round and round ;
And dusty-white with flour and meal,
  The miller whistles to its sound.

And if you listen to the rain
  When leaves and birds and bees are dumb,
You hear it pattering on the pane
  Like Andrew beating on his drum.

The coals beneath the kettle croon,
  And clap their hands and dance in glee ;
And even the kettle hums a tune
  To tell you when it's time for tea.

The world is such a happy place,
  That children, whether big or small,
Should always have a smiling face,
  And never, never sulk at all.

Gabriel Setoun.

THE OPEN AIR

Boy's Song ◇ ◇ ◇

WHERE the pools are bright and deep,
  Where the gray trout lies asleep,
Up the river and over the lea,
That's the way for Billy and me.

Where the blackbird sings the latest,
Where the hawthorn blooms the sweetest,
Where the nestlings chirp and flee,
That's the way for Billy and me.

Where the mowers mow the cleanest,
Where the hay lies thick and greenest,
There to track the homeward bee,
That's the way for Billy and me.

Where the hazel bank is steepest,
Where the shadow falls the deepest,
Where the clustering nuts fall free,
That's the way for Billy and me.*

James Hogg.

* Two stanzas omitted.

THE WEATHER

A Weather Rule   ∽   ∽   ∽

I F the evening's red and the morning gray,
   It is the sign of a bonnie day ;
If the evening's gray and the morning's red,
The lamb and the ewe will go wet to bed.

Old Rhyme.

The Prophets of the Hive   ∽   ∽

I F bees stay at home,
   Rain will soon come ;
If they fly away,
Fine will be the day.

Old Rhyme.

Good Tidings   ∽   ∽   ∽   ∽

A SUNSHINY shower
   Won't last half an hour.

R AIN before seven,
   Fine by eleven.

Old Rhymes.

Two Promises ᴄ ᴄ ᴄ

CANDLEMAS (February 2)

IF Candlemas Day be fair and bright,
  Winter will have another flight;
If on Candlemas Day it be shower and rain,
Winter is gone and will not come again.

ST. SWITHIN (July 15)

ST. Swithin's Day, if thou dost rain,
  For forty days it will remain:
St. Swithin's Day, if thou be fair.
For forty days 'twill rain nae mair.

Old Rhymes.

Signs of Foul Weather ᴄ ᴄ

THE hollow winds begin to blow;
  The clouds look black, the glass is low;
The soot falls down, the spaniels sleep;
And spiders from their cobwebs peep.
Last night the sun went pale to bed;
The moon in halos hid her head.
The boding shepherd heaves a sigh,
For. see, a rainbow spans the sky.

The walls are damp, the ditches smell,
Closed is the pink-eyed pimpernel.
Hark! how the chairs and tables crack,
Old Betty's joints are on the rack:
Her corns with shooting-pains torment her,
And to her bed untimely sent her.
Loud quack the ducks, the sea-fowl cry,
The distant hills are looking nigh.
How restless are the snorting swine!
The busy flies disturb the kine.
Low o'er the grass the swallow wings,
The cricket, too, how sharp he sings!
Puss on the hearth, with velvet paws,
Sits wiping o'er her whisker'd jaws.
The smoke from chimneys right ascends,
Then spreading, back to earth it bends.
The wind unsteady veers around,
Or settling in the South is found.
Through the clear stream the fishes rise,
And nimbly catch the incautious flies.
The glow-worms num'rous, clear and bright,
Illum'd the dewy hill last night.
At dusk the squalid toad was seen,
Like quadruped, stalk o'er the green.
The whirling wind the dust obeys,
And in the rapid eddy plays.
The frog has chang'd his yellow vest,
And in a russet coat is drest.
The sky is green, the air is still,
The mellow blackbird's voice is shrill.
The dog, so alter'd in his taste,
Quits mutton-bones, on grass to feast,
Behold the rooks, how odd their flight,

They imitate the gliding kite,
And seem precipitate to fall,
As if they felt the piercing ball.
The tender colts on back do lie,
Nor heed the traveller passing by.
In fiery red the sun doth rise,
Then wades through clouds to mount the skies.

'Twill surely rain, we see't with sorrow,
No working in the fields to-morrow.

Dr. Jenner

THE WINDS

The Four Winds ❬ ❬ ❬

THE South wind brings wet weather,
    The North wind wet and cold together;
The West wind always brings us rain,
The East wind blows it back again.

Old Rhyme.

The Wind in a Frolic ❬ ❬

THE wind one morning sprang up from sleep,
    Saying, " Now for a frolic ! now for a leap !
Now for a madcap galloping chase !
I'll make a commotion in every place ! "

So it swept with a bustle right through a great town,
Cracking the signs and scattering down
Shutters; and whisking, with merciless squalls,
Old women's bonnets and gingerbread stalls.
There never was heard a much lustier shout,
As the apples and oranges trundled about;
And the urchins that stand with their thievish eyes
For ever on watch, ran off each with a prize.

Then away to the field it went, blustering and humming,
And the cattle all wondered whatever was coming;
It plucked by the tails the grave matronly cows,
And tossed the colts' manes all over their brows;
Till, offended at such an unusual salute,
They all turned their backs, and stood sulky and mute.

So on it went capering and playing its pranks,
Whistling with reeds on the broad river's banks,
Puffing the birds as they sat on the spray,
Or the traveller grave on the king's highway.
It was not too nice to hustle the bags
Of the beggar, and flutter his dirty rags;

'Twas so bold that it feared not to play its joke
With the doctor's wig or the gentleman's cloak.
Through the forest it roared, and cried gaily, "Now,
You sturdy old oaks, I'll make you bow!"
And it made them bow without more ado,
Or it cracked their great branches through and through.

Then it rushed like a monster on cottage and farm,
Striking their dwellers with sudden alarm;
And they ran out like bees in a midsummer swarm;—

There were dames with their kerchiefs tied over their caps,
To see if their poultry were free from mishaps;
The turkeys they gobbled, the geese screamed aloud,
And the hens crept to roost in a terrified crowd;
There was rearing of ladders, and logs laying on,
Where the thatch from the roof threatened soon to be gone.

But the wind had swept on, and had met in a lane
With a schoolboy, who panted and struggled in vain;
For it tossed him and twirled him, then passed, and he stood
With his hat in a pool and his shoes in the mud.

Then away went the wind in its holiday glee,
And now it was far on the billowy sea,
And the lordly ships felt its staggering blow,
And the little boats darted to and fro.
But lo! it was night, and it sank to rest
On the sea-bird's rock in the gleaming West,
Laughing to think, in its fearful fun,
How little of mischief it really had done.

William Howitt.

Windy Nights ◇ ◇ ◇ ◇

WHENEVER the moon and stars are set,
  Whenever the wind is high,
All night long in the dark and wet,
  A man goes riding by.
Late in the night when the fires are out,
Why does he gallop and gallop about?

Whenever the trees are crying aloud,
    And ships are tossed at sea,
By, on the highway, low and loud,
    By at the gallop goes he.
By at the gallop he goes, and then
By he comes back at the gallop again.

Robert Louis Stevenson.

THE YEAR

Days of Birth ❧ ❧ ❧ ❧

MONDAY'S child is fair of face,
　　Tuesday's child is full of grace,
Wednesday's child is full of woe,
Thursday's child has far to go,
Friday's child is loving and giving,
Saturday's child works hard for its living,
And a child that's born on the Sabbath day
Is fair and wise and good and gay.

Old Rhyme.

Days of the Month ❧ ❧ ❧

THIRTY days hath September,
　　April, June, and November ;
All the rest have thirty-one ;
February twenty-eight alone,—
Except in leap-year, at which time
February's days are twenty-nine.

Old Rhyme.

The Months ∾ ∾ ∾

JANUARY brings the snow,
  Makes our feet and fingers glow.

February brings the rain,
Thaws the frozen lake again.

March brings breezes loud and shrill,
Stirs the dancing daffodil.

April brings the primrose sweet,
Scatters daisies at our feet.

May brings flocks of pretty lambs,
Skipping by their fleecy dams.

June brings tulips, lilies, roses,
Fills the children's hands with posies.

Hot July brings cooling showers,
Apricots and gillyflowers.

August brings the sheaves of corn,
Then the harvest home is borne.

Warm September brings the fruit,
Sportsmen then begin to shoot.

Fresh October brings the pheasant,
Then to gather nuts is pleasant.

Dull November brings the blast,
Then the leaves are whirling fast.

Chill December brings the sleet,
Blazing fire and Christmas treat.

Old Rhyme.

Pippa's Song ∾ ∾ ∾ ∾

THE year's at the spring
  And day's at the morn ;
Morning's at seven ;
The hill-side's dew-pearled ;
The lark's on the wing ;
The snail's on the thorn ;
God's in his heaven—
All's right with the world.

Robert Browning.

The First of May ∾ ∾ ∾

THE fair maid who, the First of May,
  Goes to the fields at break of day,
And washes in dew from the hawthorn tree,
Will ever after handsome be.

Old Rhyme.

Oxfordshire Children's May Song ∾

SPRING is coming, spring is coming,
  Birdies, build your nest ;
Weave together straw and feather,
  Doing each your best.

Spring is coming, spring is coming,
  Flowers are coming too :
Pansies, lilies, daffodillies,
  Now are coming through.

Spring is coming, spring is coming,
   All around is fair ;
Shimmer and quiver on the river,
   Joy is everywhere.

We wish you a happy May.

Country Rhyme.

Child's Song in Spring

THE silver birch is a dainty lady,
   She wears a satin gown ;
The elm tree makes the old churchyard shady,
   She will not live in town.

The English oak is a sturdy fellow,
   He gets his green coat late ;
The willow is smart in a suit of yellow,
   While brown the beech trees wait.

Such a gay green gown God gives the larches—
   As green as He is good !
The hazels hold up their arms for arches
   When Spring rides through the wood.

The chestnut's proud, and the lilac's pretty,
   The poplar's gentle and tall,
But the plane tree's kind to the poor dull city—
   I love him best of all !

E. Nesbit.

Baby Seed Song ∾ ∾ ∾ ∾

LITTLE brown brother, oh! little brown brother,
  Are you awake in the dark ?
Here we lie cosily, close to each other :
  Hark to the song of the lark—
"Waken !" the lark says, "waken and dress you ;
  Put on your green coats and gay,
Blue sky will shine on you, sunshine caress you—
  Waken ! 'tis morning—'tis May ! "

Little brown brother, oh! little brown brother,
  What kind of flower will you be ?
I'll be a poppy—all white, like my mother ;
  Do be a poppy like me.
What ! you're a sun-flower ? How I shall miss you
  When you're grown golden and high !
But I shall send all the bees up to kiss you ;
  Little brown brother, good-bye.

                                        E. Nesbit.

Two Apple-Howling Songs ∾ ∾

Sung in Orchards by the Apple-Howlers on Twelfth Day

I. SURREY

HERE stands a good apple tree.
  Stand fast at root.
Bear well at top ;
Every little twig
Bear an apple big ;

Every little bough
Bear an apple now ;
Hats full ! caps full !
Threescore sacks full !
Hullo, boys ! hullo !

II. DEVONSHIRE

HERE'S to thee, old apple tree,
   Whence thou may'st bud, and whence thou may'st blow,
And whence thou may'st bear apples enow !
   Hats full ! Caps full !
   Bushel—bushel—sacks full,
   Old parson's breeches full,
   And my pockets full too !
      Huzza !

Old Rhymes.

Mine Host of " The Golden Apple "

A GOODLY host one day was mine,
   A Golden Apple his only sign,
That hung from a long branch, ripe and fine.

My host was the bountiful apple tree ;
He gave me shelter and nourished me
With the best of fare, all fresh and free.

And light-winged guests came not a few,
To his leafy inn, and sipped the dew,
And sang their best songs ere they flew.

I slept at night, on a downy bed
Of moss, and my Host benignly spread
His own cool shadow over my head.

When I asked what reckoning there might be,
He shook his broad boughs cheerily :—
A blessing be thine, green Apple-tree !

Thomas Westwood.

The Holly ❧ ❧ ❧ ❧ ❧

A Christmas Chant

NOW of all the trees by the King's highway,
    Which do you love the best ?
O ! the one that is green upon Christmas Day,
    The bush with the bleeding breast.
Now the holly with her drops of blood for me :
For that is our dear Aunt Mary's tree.*

Its leaves are sweet with our Saviour's Name,
    'Tis a plant that loves the poor :
Summer and Winter it shines the same,
    Beside the cottage door.
O ! the holly with her drops of blood for me :
For that is our kind Aunt Mary's tree.

'Tis a bush that the birds will never leave :
    They sing in it all day long ;
But sweetest of all upon Christmas Eve,
    Is to hear the robin's song.
'Tis the merriest sound upon earth and sea :
For it comes from our own Aunt Mary's tree.

* See note, p. 318.

So, of all that grow by the King's highway,
 I love that tree the best ;
'Tis a bower for the birds upon Christmas Day,
 The bush of the bleeding breast.
O ! the holly with her drops of blood for me :
For that is our sweet Aunt Mary's tree.

       R. S. Hawker.

A Winter Song   ∾   ∾   ∾

WHEN icicles hang by the wall,
 And Dick the shepherd blows his nail,
And Tom bears logs into the hall,
 And milk comes frozen home in pail,
When blood is nipt, and ways be foul,
Then nightly sings the staring owl,
     Tuwhoo!
Tuwhit ! tuwhoo ! A merry note,
While greasy Joan doth keel the pot.

When all aloud the wind doth blow,
 And coughing drowns the parson's saw,
And birds sit brooding in the snow,
 And Marian's nose looks red and raw,
When roasted crabs hiss in the bowl,
Then nightly sings the staring owl,
     Tuwhoo!
Tuwhit ! tuwhoo ! A merry note,
While greasy Joan doth keel the pot.

      William Shakespeare.

Old Winter ◇ ◇ ◇ ◇

OLD Winter sad, in snow yclad,
    Is making a doleful din ;
But let him howl till he crack his jowl,
    We will not let him in.

Ay, let him lift from the billowy drift
    His hoary, haggard form,
And scowling stand, with his wrinkled hand
    Outstretching to the storm.

And let his weird and sleety beard
    Stream loose upon the blast,
And, rustling, chime to the tinkling rime
    From his bald head falling fast.

Let his baleful breath shed blight and death
    On herb and flower and tree ;
And brooks and ponds in crystal bonds
    Bind fast, but what care we ?

Let him push at the door,—in the chimney roar,
    And rattle the window pane ;
Let him in at us spy with his icicle eye,
    But he shall not entrance gain.

Let him gnaw, forsooth, with his freezing tooth,
    On our roof-tiles, till he tire ;
But we care not a whit, as we jovial sit
    Before our blazing fire.

Come, lads, let's sing, till the rafters ring;
    Come, push the can about;—
From our snug fire-side this Christmas-tide
    We'll keep old Winter out.

                    T. Noel.

Jack Frost   ∾   ∾   ∾   ∾

THE door was shut, as doors should be,
    Before you went to bed last night;
Yet Jack Frost has got in, you see,
    And left your window silver white.

He must have waited till you slept;
    And not a single word he spoke,
But pencilled o'er the panes and crept
    Away again before you woke.

And now you cannot see the hills
    Nor fields that stretch beyond the lane;
But there are fairer things than these
    His fingers traced on every pane.

Rocks and castles towering high;
    Hills and dales and streams and fields;
And knights in armour riding by,
    With nodding plumes and shining shields.

And here are little boats, and there
    Big ships with sails spread to the breeze;
And yonder, palm trees waving fair
    On islands set in silver seas.

And butterflies with gauzy wings ;
 And herds of cows and flocks of sheep ;
And fruit and flowers and all the things
 You see when you are sound asleep.

For creeping softly underneath
 The door when all the lights are out,
Jack Frost takes every breath you breathe,
 And knows the things you think about.

He paints them on the window pane
 In fairy lines with frozen steam ;
And when you wake you see again
 The lovely things you saw in dream.

Gabriel Setoun.

Snow in Town   ❦   ❦   ❦

NOTHING is quite so quiet and clean
 As snow that falls in the night ;
And isn't it jolly to jump from bed
 And find the whole world white ?

It lies on the window ledges,
 It lies on the boughs of the trees,
While sparrows crowd at the kitchen door,
 With a pitiful " If you *please ?* "

It lies on the arm of the lamp-post,
　Where the lighter's ladder goes,
And the policeman under it beats his arms,
　And stamps—to feel his toes ;

The butcher's boy is rolling a ball
　To throw at the man with coals,
And old Mrs. Ingram has fastened a piece
　Of flannel under her soles ;

No sound there is in the snowy road
　From the horses' cautious feet,
And all is hushed but the postman's knocks
　Rat-tatting down the street,

Till men come round with shovels
　To clear the snow away,—
What a pity it is that when it falls
　They never let it stay !

And while we are having breakfast
　Papa says, " Isn't it light ?
And all because of the thousands of geese
　The Old Woman plucked last night.

And if you are good," he tells us,
　" And attend to your A B C,
You may go in the garden and make a snow-man
　As big or bigger than me ! "

Rickman Mark.

CHRISTMAS

The Old English Christmas ∽ ∽

(From *Marmion*)

AND well our Christian sires of old
   Loved when the year its course had rolled,
And brought blithe Christmas back again,
With all his hospitable train.
Domestic and religious rite
Gave honour to the holy night;
On Christmas eve the bells were rung;
On Christmas eve the mass was sung:
That only night, in all the year,
Saw the stoled priest the chalice rear.
The damsel donned her kirtle sheen;
The hall was dressed with holy green;
Forth to the wood did merry-men go,
To gather in the mistletoe.
Then opened wide the Baron's hall
To vassal, tenant, serf, and all;
Power laid his rod of rule aside,
And Ceremony doffed his pride.
The heir, with roses in his shoes,
That night might village partner choose;
The Lord, underogating, share

The vulgar game of "post and pair."
All hailed, with uncontrolled delight,
And general voice, the happy night,
That to the cottage, as the crown,
Brought tidings of salvation down.

The fire, with well-dried logs supplied,
Went roaring up the chimney wide;
The huge hall-table's oaken face,
Scrubbed till it shone, the day to grace,
Bore then upon its massive board
No mark to part the squire and lord.
Then was brought in the lusty brawn
By old blue-coated serving-man;
Then the grim boar's-head frowned on high,
Crested with bays and rosemary.
Well can the green-garbed ranger tell,
How, when, and where, the monster fell;
What dogs before his death he tore,
And all the baiting of the boar.
The wassel round, in good brown bowls,
Garnished with ribbons, blithely trowls.
There the huge sirloin reeked; hard by
Plum-porridge stood, and Christmas pie;
Nor failed old Scotland to produce
At such high tide, her savoury goose.
Then came the merry masquers in,
And carols roared with blithesome din;
If unmelodious was the song,
It was a hearty note, and strong.
Who lists may in their mumming see
Traces of ancient mystery;
White shirts supplied the masquerade,

And smutted cheeks the visors made;
But, O! what masquers, richly dight,
Can boast of bosoms half so light!
England was merry England, when
Old Christmas brought his sports again.
'Twas Christmas broached the mightiest ale;
'Twas Christmas told the merriest tale;
A Christmas gambol oft could cheer
The poor man's heart through half the year.

Sir Walter Scott.

Three Old Carols ∽ ∽ ∽ ∽

I. THE FIRST NOWELL

THE first Nowell the Angel did say,
   Was to three poor shepherds in fields as they lay;
In fields where they lay keeping their sheep
In a cold winter's night that was so deep.
   Nowell, Nowell, Nowell, Nowell,
   Born is the King of Israel.

They lookèd up and saw a star
Shining in the East beyond them far,
And to the earth it gave great light,
And so it continued both day and night.
      Nowell, Nowell—

And by the light of that same star,
Three Wise Men came from country far.

D

To seek for a King was their intent,
And to follow the star wherever it went.
          Nowell, Nowell—

The star drew nigh to the north-west,
O'er Bethlehem it took its rest,
And there it did both stop and stay
Right over the place where Jesus lay.
          Nowell, Nowell—

Then did they know assuredly
Within that house the King did lie;
One entered in then for to see,
And found the babe in poverty.
          Nowell, Nowell—

Then entered in those Wise Men three
Most reverently upon their knee,
And offered there in His presence
Both gold, and myrrh, and frankincense.
          Nowell, Nowell—

Between an ox stall and an ass,
This child truly there born He was;
For want of clothing they did Him lay
In the manger, among the hay.
          Nowell, Nowell—

Then let us all with one accord
Sing praises to our heavenly Lord,
That hath made heaven and earth of nought,
And with His blood mankind hath bought.
          Nowell, Nowell—

If we in our time shall do well,
We shall be free from death and Hell,
For God hath prepared for us all
A resting-place in general.
    Nowell, Nowell, Nowell, Nowell,
    Born is the King of Israel.

                                    Old Carol.

II. A VIRGIN MOST PURE ∽ ∽

A VIRGIN most pure, as the prophets do tell,
    Hath brought forth a babe, as it hath her befell,
To be our Redeemer from death, hell, and sin,
Which Adam's transgression hath wrapt us all in.
    Rejoice and be merry, set sorrow aside,
    Christ Jesus, our Saviour, was born at this tide.

In Bethlehem city, in Jewry it was,
Where Joseph and Mary together did pass,
And there to be taxed, with many one mo',
For Cæsar commanded the same should be so.
    Rejoice and be merry—

But, when they had entered the city so fair,
The number of people so mighty was there,
That Joseph and Mary, whose substance was small,
Could get in the city no lodging at all.
    Rejoice and be merry—

Then they were constrain'd in a stable to lie,
Where oxen and asses they usèd to tie;
Their lodging so simple, they held it no scorn,
But against the next morning our Saviour was born.
Rejoice and be merry—

The King of all Glory to the world being brought,
Small store of fine linen to wrap him was wrought;
When Mary had swaddled her young son so sweet,
Within an ox manger she laid him to sleep.
Rejoice and be merry—

Then God sent an angel from Heaven so high,
To certain poor Shepherds in fields where they lie,
And bid them no longer in sorrow to stay,
Because that our Saviour was born on this day.
Rejoice and be merry—

Then presently after, the Shepherds did spy
A number of Angels appear in the sky,
Who joyfully talked, and sweetly did sing,
"To God be all glory, our Heavenly King."
Rejoice and be merry—

Three certain wise Princes, they thought it most meet
To lay their rich off'rings at our Saviour's feet;
Then the Shepherds consent, and to Bethlehem did go,
And when they came thither they found it was so.
Rejoice and be merry, set sorrow aside,
Christ Jesus, our Saviour, was born at this tide.
Old Carol.

III. God Rest You, Merry Gentlemen

GOD rest you, merry gentlemen,
   Let nothing you dismay,
For Jesus Christ, our Saviour,
   Was born upon this day,
To save us all from Satan's pow'r
   When we were gone astray.
      O tidings of comfort and joy!
      For Jesus Christ, our Saviour,
      Was born on Christmas Day.

In Bethlehem, in Jewry,
   This blessed babe was born,
And laid within a manger,
   Upon this blessed morn;
The which His mother, Mary,
   Nothing did take in scorn.
      O tidings—

From God our Heavenly Father,
   A blessed angel came;
And unto certain shepherds
   Brought tidings of the same:
How that in Bethlehem was born
   The Son of God by name.
      O tidings—

"Fear not," then said the angel,
   "Let nothing you affright,
This day is born a Saviour
   Of virtue, power, and might,

So frequently to vanquish all
 The friends of Satan quite."
   O tidings —

The shepherds at those tidings
 Rejoicèd much in mind,
And left their flocks a-feeding
 In tempest, storm, and wind,
And went to Bethlehem straightway,
 This blessed babe to find.
   O tidings—

But when to Bethlehem they came,
 Whereat this infant lay,
They found Him in a manger,
 Where oxen feed on hay,
His mother Mary kneeling,
 Unto the Lord did pray,
   O tidings—

Now to the Lord sing praises,
 All you within this place,
And with true love and brotherhood
 Each other now embrace;
This holy tide of Christmas
 All others doth deface.
  O tidings of comfort and joy!
  For Jesus Christ, our Saviour,
  Was born on Christmas Day.

      Old Carol.

A Song of Saint Francis   ⌒   ⌒   ⌒

THERE was a Knight of Bethlehem,
   Whose wealth was tears and sorrows;
His men-at-arms were little lambs,
   His trumpeters were sparrows.
His castle was a wooden cross,
   On which He hung so high;
His helmet was a crown of thorns,
   Whose crest did touch the sky.

          Henry Neville Maugham.

Santa Claus   ⌒   ⌒   ⌒   ⌒

HE comes in the night! He comes in the night!
   He softly, silently comes;
While the little brown heads on the pillows so white
   Are dreaming of bugles and drums.
He cuts through the snow like a ship through the foam,
   While the white flakes around him whirl;
Who tells him I know not, but he findeth the home
   Of each good little boy and girl.

His sleigh it is long, and deep, and wide;
   It will carry a host of things,
While dozens of drums hang over the side,
   With the sticks sticking under the strings.
And yet not the sound of a drum is heard,
   Not a bugle blast is blown,
As he mounts to the chimney-top like a bird,
   And drops to the hearth like a stone.

The little red stockings he silently fills,
  Till the stockings will hold no more ;
The bright little sleds for the great snow hills
  Are quickly set down on the floor.
Then Santa Claus mounts to the roof like a bird,
  And glides to his seat in the sleigh ;
Not the sound of a bugle or drum is heard
  As he noiselessly gallops away.

He rides to the East, and he rides to the West,
  Of his goodies he touches not one ;
He eateth the crumbs of the Christmas feast
  When the dear little folks are done.
Old Santa Claus doeth all that he can ;
  This beautiful mission is his ;
Then, children, be good to the little old man,
  When you find who the little man is.

Anon.

THE COUNTRY LIFE

The Farmer's Round 〜

FIRST comes January,
   The sun lies very low :
I see in the farmer's yard
   The cattle feed on stro' ;
The weather being so cold,
   The snow lies on the ground.
There will be another change of moon
   Before the year comes round.

Next is February,
   So early in the spring :
The farmer ploughs the fallows,
   The rooks their nests begin.
The little lambs appearing
   Now frisk in pretty play ;
I think upon the increase,
   And thank my God, to-day.

March it is the next month,
   So cold and hard and drear :
Prepare we now for harvest,
   By brewing of strong beer.

God grant that we who labour
  May see the reaping come,
And drink and dance and welcome
  The happy Harvest Home.

Next of months is April,
  When early in the morn
The cheery farmer soweth
  To right and left the corn.
The gallant team come after,
  A-smoothing of the land.
May Heaven the farmer prosper
  Whate'er he takes in hand.

In May I go a-walking
  To hear the linnets sing,
The blackbird and the throstle
  A-praising God the King.
It cheers the heart to hear them,
  To see the leaves unfold,
The meadows scattered over
  With buttercups of gold.

Full early in the morning
  Awakes the summer sun,
The month of June arriving,
  The cold and night are done.
The Cuckoo is a fine bird,
  She whistles as she flies,
And as she whistles "Cuckoo"
  The bluer grow the skies.

Six months I now have named,
  The seventh is July.
Come, lads and lasses, gather
  The scented hay to dry,
All full of mirth and gladness
  To turn it in the sun,
And never cease till daylight sets,
  And all the work is done.

August brings the harvest :
  The reapers now advance,
Against their shining sickles
  The field stands little chance.
"Well done ! " exclaims the farmer,
  " This day is all men's friend ;
We'll drink and feast in plenty
  When we the harvest end."

By middle of September,
  The rake is laid aside,
The horses wear the breeching,
  Rich dressing to provide ;
All things to do in season,
  Methinks is just and right.
Now summer season's over,
  The frosts begin at night.

October leads in winter,
  The leaves begin to fall,
The trees will soon be naked,
  No flowers left at all :
The frosts will bite them sharply,
  The elm alone is green ;

In orchard piles of apples red
  For cider press are seen.

The eleventh month, November,
  The nights are cold and long,
By day we're felling timber,
  And spend the night in song.
In cozy chimney corner
  We take our toast and ale,
And kiss and tease the maidens,
  Or tell a merry tale.

Then comes dark December,
  The last of months in turn:
With holly, box, and laurel
  We house and church adorn.
So now, to end my story,
  I wish you all good cheer,
A merry, happy Christmas,
  A prosperous New Year.

Old Song.

A Summer Evening *

DOWN the deep, the miry lane,
  Creaking comes the empty wain;
And driver on the shaft-horse sits,
Whistling now and then by fits;
And oft with his accustomed call,
Urging on the sluggish Ball.

* A fragment.

The barn is still, the master's gone,
And thresher puts his jacket on,
While Dick upon the ladder tail,
Nails the dead kite to the wall.
Here comes shepherd Jack at last,
He has penned the sheep-cote fast ;
For 'twas but two nights before,
A lamb was eaten on the moor ;
His empty wallet Rover carries,
Nor for Jack, when near home, tarries ;
With lolling tongue he runs to try
If the horse trough be not dry.
The milk is settled in the pans
And supper messes in the cans ;
In the hovel carts are wheeled,
And both the colts are drove a-field ;
The horses are all bedded up,
And the ewe is with the tup ;
The snare for Mister Fox is set,
The leaven laid, the thatching wet ;
And Bess has slinked away to talk
With Roger in the Holly Walk.
Now, on the settle all but Bess
Are set to eat their supper mess ;
And little Tom and roguish Kate
Are swinging on the meadow-gate.
Now they chat on various things,
Of taxes, ministers, and kings,
Or else tell all the village news,
How madam did the squire refuse ;
How parson on his tithes was bent,
And landlord oft distrained for rent.
Thus do they talk, till in the sky

The pale-eyed moon is mounted high.

. . . . . .

The mistress sees that lazy Kate
The happing coal on kitchen grate
Has laid—while master goes throughout,
Sees shutters fast, the mastiff out,
The candles safe, the hearths all clear,
And naught from thieves or fire to fear ;
Then both to bed together creep,
And join the general troop of sleep.

H. Kirke White.

The Useful Plough ∽ ∽

A COUNTRY life is sweet !
  In moderate cold and heat,
To walk in the air, how pleasant and fair !
  In every field of wheat,
  The fairest of flowers adorning the bowers,
  And every meadow's brow ;
To that I say, no courtier may
Compare with they who clothe in gray,
  And follow the useful plough.

  They rise with the morning lark,
  And labour till almost dark,
Then folding their sheep, they hasten to sleep ;
  While every pleasant park
Next morning is ringing with birds that are singing

On each green, tender bough.
With what content and merriment
Their days are spent, whose minds are bent
  To follow the useful plough !*

Old Song.

The Water-Mill

" A NY grist for the mill ? "
      How merrily it goes !
Flap, flap, flap, flap,
  While the water flows.
Round-about, and round-about,
  The heavy mill-stones grind,
And the dust flies all about the mill,
  And makes the miller blind.

" Any grist for the mill ? "
  The jolly farmer packs
His waggon with a heavy load
  Of very heavy sacks.
Noisily, oh noisily,
  The mill-stones turn about :
You cannot make the miller hear
  Unless you scream and shout.

" Any grist for the mill ? "
  The bakers come and go ;

---

* Other lines omitted.

E

They bring their empty sacks to fill,
  And leave them down below.
The dusty miller and his men
  Fill all the sacks they bring,
And while they go about their work
  Right merrily they sing.

"Any grist for the mill?"
  How quickly it goes round!
Splash, splash, splash, splash,
  With a whirring sound.
Farmers, bring your corn to-day;
  And bakers, buy your flour;
Dusty millers, work away,
  While it is in your power.

"Any grist for the mill?"
  Alas! it will not go;
The river, too, is standing still,
  The ground is white with snow.
And when the frosty weather comes,
  And freezes up the streams,
The miller only hears the mill
  And grinds the corn in dreams.

Living close beside the mill,
  The miller's girls and boys
Always play at make-believe,
  Because they have no toys.
"Any grist for our mill?"
  The elder brothers shout,
While all the little Petticoats
  Go whirling round about.

The miller's little boys and girls
   Rejoice to see the snow.
"Good father, play with us to-day;
   You cannot work, you know.
We will be the mill-stones,
   And you shall be the wheel;
We'll pelt each other with the snow,
   And it shall be the meal."

Oh, heartily the miller's wife
   Is laughing at the door :
She never saw the mill worked
   So merrily before.
"Bravely done, my little lads,
   Rouse up the lazy wheel,
For money comes but slowly in
   When snow-flakes are the meal."

                                    "Aunt Effie."

The Windmill

BEHOLD! a giant am I !
   Aloft here in my tower,
   With my granite jaws I devour
The maize, and the wheat, and the rye,
   And grind them into flour.

I look down over the farms ;
   In the fields of grain I see
   The harvest that is to be,
And I fling to the air my arms,
   For I know it is all for me.

I hear the sound of flails
 Far off, from the threshing-floors
 In barns, with their open doors,
And the wind, the wind in my sails,
 Louder and louder roars.

I stand here in my place
 With my foot on the rock below,
 And whichever way it may blow,
I meet it face to face
 As a brave man meets his foe.

And while we wrestle and strive,
 My master, the miller, stands
 And feeds me with his hands;
For he knows who makes him thrive,
 Who makes him lord of lands.

On Sundays I take my rest;
 Church-going bells begin
 Their low melodious din;
I cross my arms on my breast,
 And all is peace within.

H. W. Longfellow.

The Castle-Builder ∾ ∾

IT happened on a summer's day,
  A country lass as fresh as May,
Decked in a wholesome russet gown,
Was going to the market town ;
So blithe her looks, so simply clean,
You'd take her for a May-day queen ;
Though for her garland, says the tale,
Her head sustained a loaded pail.
As on her way she passed along,
She hummed the fragments of a song ;
She did not hum for want of thought—
Quite pleased with what to sale she brought,
She reckoned by her own account,
When all was sold, the whole amount.
Thus she—" In time this little ware
May turn to great account, with care :
My milk being sold for—so and so,
I'll buy some eggs as markets go,
And set them ;—at the time I fix,
These eggs will bring as many chicks ;
I'll spare no pains to feed them well ;
They'll bring vast profit when they sell.
With this, I'll buy a little pig,
And when 'tis grown up fat and big,
I'll sell it, whether boar or sow,
And with the money buy a cow :
This cow will surely have a calf,
And there the profit's half in half ;
Besides there's butter, milk, and cheese,
To keep the market when I please :
All which I'll sell, and buy a farm,

Then shall of sweethearts have a swarm.
Oh! then for ribands, gloves, and rings!
Ay! more than twenty pretty things—
One brings me this, another that,
And I shall have—I know not what!"

Fired with the thought—the sanguine lass!—
Of what was thus to come to pass,
Her heart beat strong; she gave a bound,
And down came milk-pail on the ground:
Eggs, fowls, pig, hog (ah, well-a-day!)
Cow, calf, and farm—all swam away!

La Fontaine (translated).

John Barleycorn ∾ ∾ ∾

THERE were three kings into the East,
 Three kings both great and high,
And they ha'e sworn a solemn oath
 John Barleycorn should die.

They took a plough and plough'd him down,
 Put clods upon his head;
And they ha'e sworn a solemn oath,
 John Barleycorn was dead.

But the cheerful spring came kindly on,
 And show'rs began to fall;
John Barleycorn got up again,
 And sore surpris'd them all.

The sultry suns óf summer came,
   And he grew thick and strong;
His head weel arm'd wi' pointed spears,
   That no one should him wrong.

The sober autumn enter'd mild,
   When he grew wan and pale;
His bending joints and drooping head
   Show'd he began to fail.

His colour sickened more and more,
   He faded unto age;
And then his enemies began
   To show their deadly rage.

They've ta'en a weapon, long and sharp,
   And cut him by the knee;
And tied him fast upon the cart,
   Like a rogue for forgerie.

They laid him down upon his back,
   And cudgell'd him full sore;
They hung him up before the storm,
   And turn'd him o'er and o'er.

They filled up a darksome pit
   With water to the brim;
They heaved in John Barleycorn,
   There let him sink or swim.

They laid him out upon the floor,
   To work him further woe:
And still, as signs of life appear'd,
   They toss'd him to and fro.

They wasted o'er a scorching flame
   The marrow of his bones;
But a miller us'd him worst of all—
   He crush'd him 'tween two stones.

And they ha'e ta'en his very heart's blood,
   And drank it round and round;
And still the more and more they drank,
   Their joy did more abound.

John Barleycorn was a hero bold,
   Of noble enterprise;
For if you do but taste his blood,
   'Twill make your courage rise.

'Twill make a man forget his woe;
   'Twill heighten all his joy:
'Twill make the widow's heart to sing,
   Tho' the tear were in her eye.

Then let us toast John Barleycorn,
   Each man a glass in hand;
And may his great posterity
   Ne'er fail in old Scotland.

Robert Burns.

Oxfordshire Guy Fawkes' Song ᔕ   ᔕ   ᔕ

REMEMBER, remember
   The Fifth of November.
 Bonfire Night—
We want a faggot
   To make it alight.
Hatchets and duckets,
   Beetles and wedges,
If you don't give us some,
   We'll pull your old hedges ;
If you don't give us one,
   We'll take two :
The better for us
   And the worse for you !

Country Rhyme.

The Cricket Bat Sings   ᔕ   ᔕ   ᔕ   ᔕ

WILLOW and cane is all I am, with a wisp of waxen
      thread,
Cane and willow, willow and cane, fondly, perfectly wed ;
But never wood for a bounding yacht was picked with a
      nicer thought,
And nothing planned by human hand ever was deftlier
      wrought.
Willow and cane is all I am ; but here is a wondrous thing:
Willow and cane is all I am, yet also am I a king !

The flower of the earth my subjects are, and the throne
    of the cricket bat
Is the rich, green turf of a level mead, and who has a
    throne like that?

A century old is the crown I hold; nothing disturbs my
    reign;
And men to me will bend the knee while centuries more
    shall wane;
The Sword is great, but he rules by hate, rules with a
    bloody hand:
Honesty, peace, and comradeship are features of my
    command!
Scour the earth and you shall not find the like of the
    power I wield,
For the home of the brave, the strong, the free, is the
    elm-girt cricket-field;
Both man and boy they thrill with joy to speed the ball
    away—
Willow and cane is all I am, yet look at the hosts I sway!

From " Songs of the Bat."

Golden Rules for the Young ❧

IN batting, hold your bat upright,
    Play every ball with all your might.

In bowling, never exceed your strength,
Keep straight, but vary pace and length.

In fielding, put two hands to the ball:
A butter-fingers is worst of all.

From " The Boy's Own Paper."

A Hunting Song ∽ ∽ ∽

THE dusky night rides down the sky,
    And ushers in the morn;
The hounds all join in glorious cry,
    The huntsman winds his horn.
            Then a-hunting we will go.

The wife around her husband throws
    Her arms, and begs him stay;
"My dear, it rains, it hails, it snows,
    You will not hunt to-day?"
            But a-hunting we will go.

A brushing fox in yonder wood,
    Secure to find we seek:
For why, I carried, sound and good,
    A cartload there last week.
            And a-hunting we will go.

Away he goes, he flies the rout,
    Their steeds all spur and switch,
Some are thrown in, and some thrown out,
    And some thrown in the ditch.
            But a-hunting we will go.

At length his strength to faintness worn,
    Poor Reynard ceases fight;
Then hungry, homeward we return,
    To feast away the night.
            Then a-drinking we do go.

                    Henry Fielding.

A Skating Song ～ ～ ～

AWAY! away! our fires stream bright
　　Along the frozen river;
And their arrowy sparkles of frosty light
　　On the forest branches quiver.
Away! away! for the stars are forth,
　　And on the pure snows of the valley,
In a giddy trance, the moonbeams dance—
　　Come, let us our comrades rally!

Away! away! o'er the sheeted ice,
　　Away, away we go;
On our steel-bound feet we move as fleet
　　As deer o'er the Lapland snow.
What though the sharp north winds are out,
　　The skater heeds them not—
'Midst the laugh and shout of the jocund rout,
　　Gray winter is forgot.*

Let others choose more gentle sports,
　　By the side of the winter hearth;
Or 'neath the lamps of the festal halls,
　　Seek for their share of mirth;
But as for me, away! away!
　　Where the merry skaters be—
Where the fresh wind blows, and the smooth ice glows,
　　There is the place for me.

Ephraim Peabody.

* One stanza omitted.

BLOSSOMS FROM
HERRICK AND BLAKE

A Grace for a Child ∾ ∾

HERE a little child I stand,
    Heaving up my either hand ;
Cold as Paddocks * though they be,
Here I lift them up to Thee,
For a Benizon to fall
On our meat, and on us all. *Amen.*

                              Robert Herrick.

A Ternarie of Littles, upon a
Pipkin of Jellie sent to a Lady ∾

A LITTLE Saint best fits a little Shrine,
    A little Prop best fits a little Vine,
As my small Cruse best fits my little Wine.

A little Seed best fits a little Soyle,
A little Trade best fits a little Toyle,
As my small Jarre best fits my little Oyle.

A little Bin best fits a little Bread,
A little Garland fits a little Head,
As my small Stuffe best fits my little Shed.

                        * Frogs.

A little Hearth best fits a little Fire,
A little Chappell fits a little Quire,
As my small Bell best fits my little Spire.

A little Stream best fits a little Boat,
A little Lead best fits a little Float,
As my small Pipe best fits my little Note.

A little Meat best fits a little Bellie,
As sweetly, Lady, give me leave to tell ye,
This little Pipkin fits this little Jellie.

Robert Herrick.

His Grange ; or, Private Wealth

THOUGH Clock,
To tell how night drawes hence, I've none,
        A Cock
I have, to sing how day drawes on.
        I have
A maid (my *Prew*) by good luck sent,
        To save
That little, Fates me gave or lent.
        A Hen
I keep, which creeking day by day,
        Tells when
She goes her long white egg to lay.
        A Goose
I have, which, with a jealous care,
        Lets loose
Her tongue, to tell what danger's neare.

A Lamb
I keep (tame) with my morsells fed,
Whose Dam
An Orphan left him (lately dead).
A Cat
I keep, that playes about my House,
Grown fat
With eating many a miching * Mouse.
To these
A *Trasy* † I do keep, whereby
I please
The more my rurall privacie :
Which are
But toyes, to give my heart some ease :
Where care
None is, slight things do lightly please.

Robert Herrick.

Nurse's Song ᘒ   ᘒ   ᘒ   ᘒ   ᘒ

WHEN the voices of children are heard on the green,
  And laughing is heard on the hill,
My heart is at rest within my breast,
  And everything else is still.
"Then come home, my children, the sun is gone down,
  And the dews of night arise ;
Come, come, leave off play, and let us away,
  Till the morning appears in the skies."

* Pilfering.   † His spaniel.

"No, no, let us play, for it is yet day,
    And we cannot go to sleep;
Besides, in the sky the little birds fly,
    And the hills are all covered with sheep."
"Well, well, go and play till the light fades away,
    And then go home to bed."
The little ones leaped, and shouted, and laughed,
    And all the hills echoèd.

William Blake

The Shepherd ∽ ∽ ∽ ∽

HOW sweet is the shepherd's sweet lot!
    From the morn to the evening he strays;
He shall follow his sheep all the day,
And his tongue shall be filled with praise.

For he hears the lambs' innocent call,
And he hears the ewes' tender reply;
He is watchful while they are in peace,
For they know when their shepherd is nigh.

William Blake.

Infant Joy ∽ ∽ ∽ ∽

" I HAVE no name;
    I am but two days old."
"What shall I call thee?"
    " I happy am,
Joy is my name!"

" Pretty joy !
Sweet joy, but two days old.
Sweet joy I call thee ;
Thou dost smile,
I sing the while ;
Sweet joy befall thee !"

William Blake.

Holy Thursday ～ ～ ～ ～ ～

'TWAS on a Holy Thursday, their innocent faces clean,
    Came children walking two and two, in red, and
      blue, and green :
Grey-headed beadles walked before, with wands as white as
      snow,
Till into the high dome of Paul's they like Thames waters
      flow.

Oh what a multitude they seemed, these flowers of London
      town !
Seated in companies they sit, with radiance all their own.
The hum of multitudes was there, but multitudes of lambs,
Thousands of little boys and girls raising their innocent
      hands.

Now like a mighty wind they raise to heaven the voice of
      song,
Or like harmonious thunderings the seats of heaven among:
Beneath them sit the aged men, wise guardians of the poor.
Then cherish pity, lest you drive an angel from your door.
                        William Blake.

Laughing Song ⌒ ⌒ ⌒ ⌒

WHEN the green woods laugh with the voice of joy,
　　And the dimpling stream runs laughing by ;
When the air does laugh with our merry wit,
And the green hill laughs with the noise of it ;

When the meadows laugh with lively green,
And the grasshopper laughs in the merry scene ;
When Mary, and Susan, and Emily
With their sweet round mouths sing, " Ha, ha, he ! "

When the painted birds laugh in the shade,
Where our table with cherries and nuts is spread :
Come live, and be merry, and join with me,
To sing the sweet chorus of " Ha, ha, he ! "

William Blake.

BIRDS

Answer to a Child's Question ∽ ∽ ∽

DO you know what the birds say? The Sparrow, the Dove,
   The Linnet and Thrush say, "I love and I love!"
In the winter they're silent—the wind is so strong;
What it says, I don't know, but it sings a loud song.
But green leaves, and blossoms, and sunny warm weather,
And singing, and loving—all come back together.
But the Lark is so brimful of gladness and love,
The green fields below him, the blue sky above,
That he sings, and he sings, and for ever sings he—
"I love my Love and my Love loves me!"

                                   S. T. Coleridge.

A Rule for Birds' Nesters ∽ ∽ ∽ ∽

THE robin and the red-breast,
   The robin and the wren;
If ye take out o' their nest,
   Ye'll never thrive agen!

The robin and the red-breast,
   The martin and the swallow;
If ye touch one o' their eggs,
   Bad luck will surely follow!

                         Old Rhyme.

Cherries ∽ ∽ ∽ ∽ ∽

UNDER the tree the farmer said,
    Smiling and shaking his wise old head:
"Cherries are ripe! but then, you know,
There's the grass to cut and the corn to hoe;
We can gather the cherries any day,
But when the sun shines we must make our hay;
To-night, when the work has all been done,
We'll muster the boys, for fruit and fun."

Up on the tree a robin said,
Perking and cocking his saucy head,
"Cherries are ripe! and so to-day
We'll gather them while you make the hay;
For we are the boys with no corn to hoe,
No cows to milk, and no grass to mow."
At night the farmer said: "Here's a trick!
These roguish robins have had their pick."

F. E. Weatherley.

THE CUCKOO

I. The Cuckoo's Habits ∽ ∽ ∽

IN April,
    Come he will;
In May,
He sings all day;

In June,
He changes his tune;
In July,
He makes ready to fly;
In August,
Go he must.

Old Rhyme.

II. The Cuckoo's Voice ∽ ∽ ∽

IN April the koo-coo can sing her note by rote,
  In June of tune she cannot sing a note;
At first koo-koo, koo-coo, sing shrill can she do;
At last, kooke, kooke, kooke, six cookes to one koo.

John Heywood.

III. The Cuckoo's Character ∽ ∽

THE Cuckoo's a fine bird,
  He sings as he flies;
He brings us good tidings,
  He tells us no lies.

He sucks little birds' eggs,
  To make his voice clear;
And when he sings "Cuckoo!"
  The summer is near.

Old Rhyme.

IV. The Cuckoo's Wit ∽ ∽ ∽

A Cornish Folk-Song

NOW, of all the birds that keep the tree,
　　Which is the wittiest fowl?
Oh, the Cuckoo—the Cuckoo's the one!—for he
　　Is wiser than the owl!

He dresses his wife in her Sunday's best,
　　And they never have rent to pay;
For she folds her feathers in a neighbour's nest,
　　And thither she goes to lay!

He winked with his eye, and he buttoned his purse,
　　When the breeding time began;
For he'd put his children out to nurse
　　In the house of another man!

Then his child, though born in a stranger's bed,
　　Is his own true father's son;
For he gobbles the lawful children's bread,
　　And he starves them one by one!

So, of all the birds that keep the tree,
　　This is the wittiest fowl!
Oh, the Cuckoo—the Cuckoo's the one!—for he
　　Is wiser than the owl!

R. S. Hawker.

Eagles ❧ ❧ ❧ ❧ ❧ ❧ ❧

(From Introduction to *Songs of the Voices of Birds*)

MARTIN, the Boatman.   Look you now,
     This vessel's off the stocks, a tidy craft.
Child. A schooner, Martin?
Martin.   No, boy, no; a brig,
Only she's schooner-rigged—a lovely craft.
Child.   Is she for me? O, thank you, Martin dear.
What shall I call her?
Martin.   Well, sir, what you please.
Child. Then write on her "The Eagle."
Martin.   Bless the child!
Eagle! Why, you know nought of eagles, you.
When we lay off the coast, up Canada way,
And chanced to be ashore when twilight fell,
That was the place for eagles; bald they were,
With eyes as yellow as gold.
Child.   O, Martin dear,
Tell me about them.
Martin.   Tell! there's nought to tell,
Only they snored o' nights and frighted us.
Child. Snored?
Martin. Ay, I tell you, snored; they slept upright
In the great oaks by scores; as true as time,
If I'd had aught upon my mind just then,
I wouldn't have walked that wood for unknown gold;
It was most awful. When the moon was full,
I've seen them fish at night, in the middle watch,
When she got low. I've seen them plunge like stones,
And come up fighting with a fish as long,
Ay, longer than my arm; and they would sail—
When they had struck its life out—they would sail—

Over the deck, and show their fell, fierce eyes,
And croon for pleasure, hug the prey, and speed
Grand as a frigate on a wind.
   Child.   My ship,
She must be called " The Eagle " after these.

Jean Ingelow.

The Burial of the Linnet   ∽   ∽

FOUND in the garden dead in his beauty—
  Oh that a linnet should die in the spring!
Bury him, comrades, in pitiful duty,
  Muffle the dinner-bell, solemnly ring.

Bury him kindly, up in the corner;
  Bird, beast, and goldfish are sepulchred there.
Bid the black kitten march as chief mourner,
  Waving her tail like a plume in the air.

Bury him nobly—next to the donkey;
  Fetch the old banner, and wave it about;
Bury him deeply—think of the monkey,
  Shallow his grave, and the dogs get him out.

Bury him softly—white wool around him,
  Kiss his poor feathers—the first kiss and last;
Tell his poor widow kind friends have found him:
  Plant his poor grave with whatever grows fast.

Farewell, sweet singer! dead in thy beauty,
  Silent through summer, though other birds sing.
Bury him, comrades, in pitiful duty,
  Muffle the dinner-bell, mournfully ring.

Mrs. Ewing.

DOGS AND HORSES

The Perfect Greyhound ⌒ ⌒ ⌒

IF you would have a good tyke,
　Of which there are few like,—
He must be headed like a snake,
Necked like a drake,
Backed like a beam,
Sided like a bream,
Tailed like a bat,
And footed like a cat.

Old Rhyme.

Old Pincher ⌒ ⌒ ⌒ ⌒ ⌒

WHEN I gave to old Dobbin his song and his due,
　Apollo I fear'd would look scornfully blue ;
I thought he might spurn the low station and blood
And turn such a Pegasus out of his stud.

But another "four-footed" comes boldly to claim
His place beside Dobbin in merits and fame ;
He shall have it,—for why should I be over nice,
Since Homer immortalised Ilion and—mice ?

I frolick'd, a youngling, wild, rosy, and fat,
When Pincher was brought in the butcher-boy's hat ;
And the long-promised puppy was hail'd with a joy
That ne'er was inspired by a gold-purchased toy.

"What a darling ! " cried I ; while my sire, with a frown,
Exclaimed, "Hang the brute ! though 'tis easy to drown " ;
But I wept at the word, till my sorrowful wail
Won his total reprieve from the rope or the pail.

Regarding his beauty, I'm silent : forsooth,
I've a little old-fashion'd respect for the truth ;
And the praise of his colour or shape to advance
Would be that part of history known as romance.

There were some who most rudely denounced him a "cur."
How I hated that name, though I dar'd not demur !
I thought him all fair ; yet I'll answer for this,
That the fate of Narcissus could ne'er have been his.

Now Dobbin, the pony, belonged to us all ;
Was at every one's service, and every one's call :
But Pincher, rare treasure, possession divine,
Was held undisputed as whole and sole mine.

Together we rambled, together we grew.
Many plagues had the household, but we were the two
Who were branded the deepest ; all doings revil'd
Were sure to be wrought by "that dog and that child."

Unkennel'd and chainless, yet truly he served ;
No serfdom was known, yet his faith never swerved ;
A dog has a heart,—secure that, and you'll find
That *love* even in brutes is the safest to bind.

If my own kin or kind had demolish'd my ball,
The transgression were mark'd with a scuffle and squall;
But with perfect consent he might mouth it about,
Till the very last atom of sawdust was out.

When halfpence were doled for the holiday treat,
How I long'd for the comfits, so lusciously sweet:
But cakes *must* be purchased, for how could I bear
To feast on a luxury Pinch could not share?

I fondled, I fed him, I coax'd or I cuff'd,—
I drove or I led him, I sooth'd or I huff'd:
He had beatings in anger, and huggings in love;
But which were most cruel, 'twere a puzzle to prove.

If he dared to rebel, I might battle and wage
The fierce war of a tyrant with petulant rage:
I might ply him with kicks, or belabour with blows,
But Pincher was never once known to oppose.

Did a mother appear the loud quarrel to learn,
If 'twere only with him it gave little concern:
No ill-usage could rouse him, no insult could chafe;
While Pinch was the playmate, her darling was safe.

If the geese on the common gave signal of fear,
And screams most unmusical startled the ear,
The cause was soon guess'd; for my foremost delight
Was in seeing Pinch put the old gander to flight.

Had the pantry been rifled of remnant of beef,
Shrewd suspicions were form'd of receiver and thief,
For I paused not at crime, and I blush'd not at fibs
That assisted to nurture his well-cover'd ribs.

G

The warren was sacred, yet he and I dared
To career through its heath till the rabbits were scared:
The gamekeeper threaten'd me Pinch should be shot;
But the threat was by both of us always forgot.

The linen, half-bleach'd, must be rinsed o'er again;
And our footsteps in mud were "remarkably" plain.
The tulips were crush'd, to the gardener's dismay;
And when last we were seen we were bending that way.*

But we weathered all gales, and the years sped away,
Till his "bonny black" hide was fast turning to gray;
When accents were heard most alarmingly sad,
Proclaiming that Pincher, my Pincher, was mad.

It was true: his fixed doom was no longer a joke;
He that moment must die: my young heart was nigh broke.
I saw the sure fowling-piece moved from its rest,
And the sob of keen anguish burst forth unsuppress'd.

A shot,—a faint howl,—and old Pincher was dead.
How I wept while the gardener prepared his last bed:
Something fell on his spade too, wet, sparkling, and clear;
Though *he* said 'twas a dew-drop, *I* know 'twas a tear.†

Eliza Cook.

---

* A stanza omitted.
† The piece has been made to end here, but there are five more stanzas.

Poor Old Horse ∾ ∾ ∾ ∾ ∾

O ONCE I lay in stable, a hunter well and warm,
　　I had the best of shelter from cold and rain and harm ;
But now in open meadow, a hedge I'm glad to find,
To shield my sides from tempest, from driving sleet and
　　wind.
　　　　　　　　Poor old horse, let him die !

My shoulders once were sturdy, were glossy, smooth, and
　　round,
But now, alas ! they're rotten, I'm not accounted sound.
As I have grown so aged, my teeth gone to decay,
My master frowns upon me ; I often hear him say,
　　　　　　　"Poor old horse, let him die ! "

A groom upon me waited, on straw I snugly lay,
When fields were full of flowers, the air was sweet with hay ;
But now there's no good feeding prepared for me at all,
I'm forced to munch the nettles upon the kennel wall.
　　　　　　　　Poor old horse, let him die !

My shoes and skin, the huntsman that covets them shall
　　have,
My flesh and bones the hounds, sir ! I very freely give,
I've followed them full often, aye ! many a score of miles,
O'er hedges, walls, and ditches, nor blinked at gates and stiles.
　　　　　　　　Poor old horse, let him die !

Ye gentlemen of England, ye sportsmen good and bold,
All ye that love a hunter, remember him when old ;

O put him in your stable, and make the old boy warm,
And visit him and pat him, and keep him out of harm,
Poor old horse, till he die.

Old Song.

The Arab's Farewell to his Steed

MY beautiful! my beautiful! that standest meekly by
With thy proudly-arched and glossy neck, and dark
and fiery eye;
Fret not to roam the desert now with all thy wingèd speed:
I may not mount on thee again—thou'rt sold, my Arab
steed!

Fret not with that impatient hoof, snuff not the breezy
wind,—
The further that thou fliest now, so far am I behind.
The stranger hath thy bridle rein—thy master hath *his* gold;
Fleet-limbed and beautiful, farewell!—thou'rt sold, my steed,
thou'rt sold.

Farewell! Those free, untirèd limbs full many a mile
must roam,
To reach the chill and wintry sky which clouds the stranger's
home.
Some other hand, less fond, must now thy corn and bed
prepare;
The silky mane I braided once, must be another's care.

The morning sun shall dawn again, but never more with
 thee
Shall I gallop through the desert paths, where we were wont
 to be ;
Evening shall darken on the earth, and o'er the sandy plain
Some other steed, with slower step, shall bear me home
 again.

Yes, thou must go !　The wild, free breeze, the brilliant sun
 and sky,
Thy master's home—from all of these my exiled one must
 fly.
Thy proud dark eye will grow less proud, thy step become
 less fleet,
And vainly shalt thou arch thy neck thy master's hand to
 meet.

Only in sleep shall I behold that dark eye glancing bright ;
Only in sleep shall hear again that step so firm and light ;
And when I raise my dreaming arm to check or cheer thy
 speed,
Then must I, starting, wake to feel—thou'rt *sold*, my Arab
 steed !

Ah ! rudely then, unseen by me, some cruel hand may chide,
Till foam-wreaths lie, like crested waves, along thy panting
 side ;
And the rich blood that's in thee swells, in thy indignant
 pain,
Till careless eyes which rest on thee may count each starting vein.

Will they ill-use thee? If I thought—but no, it cannot be,
Thou art so swift, yet easy curbed ; so gentle, yet so free ;
And yet if haply, when thou'rt gone, my lonely heart should
    yearn,
Can the hand which casts thee from it now command thee
    to return ?

Return !—alas, my Arab steed ! what shall thy master do,
When thou, who wert his all of joy, hast vanished from his
    view ?
When the dim distance cheats mine eye, and through the
    gathering tears
Thy bright form, for a moment, like the false mirage,
    appears ?

Slow and unmounted shall I roam, with weary step alone,
Where with fleet step and joyous bound thou oft hast borne
    me on ;
And, sitting down by that green well, I'll pause and sadly
    think,
"It was *here* he bowed his glossy neck when last I saw him
    drink ! "

When last I saw him drink !—away ! the fevered dream is
    o'er !
I could not live a day and *know* that we should meet no
    more !
They tempted me, my beautiful ! for hunger's power is
    strong—
They tempted me, my beautiful ! but I have loved too long.

Who said that I had given thee up? who said that thou
    wert sold?
'Tis false!—'tis false, my Arab steed! I fling them back
    their gold!
Thus, *thus*, I leap upon thy back, and scour the distant
    plains!
Away! who overtakes us now may claim *thee* for his pains!

                       Hon. Mrs. Norton.

The Ballad of Jenny the Mare

I

I'LL sing you a song, and a merry, merry song,
    Concerning our Yorkshire Jen;
Who never yet ran with horse or mare,
    That ever she cared for a pin.

II

When first she came to Newmarket town,
    The sportsmen all view'd her around;
All the cry was, "Alas, poor wench,
    Thou never can run this ground!"

III

When they came to the starting-post,
    The Mare look'd very smart;
And let them all say what they will,
    She never lost her start.

IV

When they got to the two-mile post,
    Poor Jenny was cast behind:
She was cast behind, she was cast behind,
    All for to take her wind.

V

When they got to the three-mile post,
    The Mare look'd very pale—
SHE LAID DOWN HER EARS ON HER BONNY NECK,
    AND BY THEM ALL DID SHE SAIL;

VI

"Come follow me, come follow me,
    All you that run so neat;
And ere that you catch me again,
    I'll make you all to sweat."

VII

When she got to the winning-post,
    The people all gave a shout;
And Jenny click'd up her lily-white foot,
    And jumped like any buck.

VIII

The Jockey said to her, "This race you have run,
    This race for me you have got;
You could gallop it all over again,
    When the rest could hardly trot!"

                    From "Euphranor."

How they brought the Good News from
Ghent to Aix ☙ ☙ ☙ ☙

I SPRANG to the stirrup, and Joris, and he;
  I galloped, Dirck galloped, we galloped all three;
"Good speed!" cried the watch, as the gate-bolts undrew;
"Speed!" echoed the wall to us galloping through;
Behind shut the postern, the lights sank to rest,
And into the midnight we galloped abreast.

Not, a word to each other; we kept the great pace
Neck by neck, stride by stride, never changing our place;
I turned in my saddle and made its girths tight,
Then shortened each stirrup, and set the pique right,
Rebuckled the cheek-strap, chained slacker the bit,
Nor galloped less steadily Roland a whit.

'Twas moonset at starting; but while we drew near
Lokeren, the cocks crew and twilight dawned clear;
At Boom, a great yellow star came out to see;
At Düffeld, 'twas morning as plain as could be;
And from Mecheln church-steeple we heard the half-
    chime,
So, Joris broke silence with, "Yet there is time!"

At Aershot, up leaped of a sudden the sun,
And against him the cattle stood black every one,
To stare thro' the mist at us galloping past,
And I saw my stout galloper Roland at last,
With resolute shoulders, each butting away
The haze, as some bluff river headland its spray,

And his low head and crest, just one sharp ear bent back
For my voice, and the other pricked out on his track;
And one eye's black intelligence,—ever that glance
O'er its white edge at me, his own master, askance!
And the thick heavy spume-flakes which aye and anon
His fierce lips shook upwards in galloping on.

By Hasselt, Dirck groaned; and cried Joris, "Stay spur!
Your Roos galloped bravely, the fault's not in her,
We'll remember at Aix"—for one heard the quick wheeze
Of her chest, saw the stretched neck and staggering knees,
And sunk tail, and horrible heave of the flank,
As down on her haunches she shuddered and sank.

So we were left galloping, Joris and I,
Past Looz and past Tongres, no cloud in the sky;
The broad sun above laughed a pitiless laugh,
'Neath our feet broke the brittle bright stubble like chaff;
Till over by Dalhem a dome-spire sprang white,
And "Gallop," gasped Joris, "for Aix is in sight!"

"How they'll greet us!"—and all in a moment his roan
Rolled neck and croup over, lay dead as a stone;
And there was my Roland to bear the whole weight
Of the news which alone could save Aix from her fate,
With his nostrils like pits full of blood to the brim,
And with circles of red for his eye-sockets' rim.

Then I cast loose my buffcoat, each holster let fall,
Shook off both my jack-boots, let go belt and all,
Stood up in the stirrup, leaned, patted his ear,
Called my Roland his pet-name, my horse without peer;

Clapped my hands, laughed and sang, any noise, bad or
    good,
Till at length into Aix Roland galloped and stood.

And all I remember is—friends flocking round
As I sate with his head 'twixt my knees on the ground;
And no voice but was praising this Roland of mine,
As I poured down his throat our last measure of wine,
Which (the burgesses voted by common consent)
Was no more than his due who brought good news from
    Ghent.

Robert Browning.

Epitaph on a Hare   ∩   ∩   ∩

HERE lies, whom hound did ne'er pursue,
    Nor swifter greyhound follow,
Whose foot ne'er tainted morning dew,
    Nor ear heard huntsman's hallo,

Old Tiney, surliest of his kind,
    Who, nurs'd with tender care,
And to domestic bounds confin'd,
    Was still a wild Jack-hare.

Though duly from my hand he took
    His pittance ev'ry night,
He did it with a jealous look,
    And, when he could, would bite.

His diet was of wheaten bread,
    And milk, and oats, and straw ;
Thistles, or lettuces instead,
    With sand to scour his maw.

On twigs of hawthorn he regal'd,
    On pippins' russet peel,
And, when his juicy salads fail'd,
    Slic'd carrot pleas'd him well.

A Turkey carpet was his lawn,
    Whereon he lov'd to bound,
To skip and gambol like a fawn,
    And swing his rump around.

His frisking was at ev'ning hours,
    For then he lost his fear,
But most before approaching show'rs,
    Or when a storm drew near.

Eight years and five round-rolling moons
    He thus saw steal away,
Dozing out all his idle noons,
    And ev'ry night at play.

I kept him for his humour's sake,
    For he would oft beguile
My heart of thoughts, that made it ache,
    And force me to a smile.

But now beneath this walnut shade
    He finds his long last home,
And waits in snug concealment laid,
    Till gentler Puss shall come.

He still more aged feels the shocks,
   From which no care can save,
And, partner once of Tiney's box,
   Must soon partake his grave.

                               William Cowper.

The Tiger   ∾   ∾   ∾

TIGER, tiger, burning bright
   In the forests of the night,
What immortal hand or eye
Could frame thy fearful symmetry?

In what distant deeps or skies
Burnt the fire of thine eyes?
On what wings dare he aspire?
What the hand dare seize thy fire?

And what shoulder and what art
Could twist the sinews of thy heart?
And when thy heart began to beat,
What dread hand formed thy dread feet?

What the hammer? what the chain?
In what furnace was thy brain?
What the anvil? what dread grasp
Dare its deadly terrors clasp?

When the stars threw down their spears,
And watered heaven with their tears,

Did He smile His work to see?
Did He who made the lamb make thee?

Tiger, tiger, burning bright
In the forests of the night,
What immortal hand or eye
Dare frame thy fearful symmetry?

William Blake.

COMPRESSED NATURAL
HISTORY

Birds, Beasts, and Fishes ∽

THE Dog will come when he is called,
　　The Cat will walk away,
The Monkey's cheek is very bald,
　The Goat is fond of play.
The Parrot is a prate-apace,
　Yet knows not what he says ;
The noble Horse will win the race,
　Or draw you in a chaise.

The Pig is not a feeder nice,
　The Squirrel loves a nut,
The Wolf would eat you in a trice,
　The Buzzard's eyes are shut.
The Lark sings high up in the air,
　The Linnet in the tree ;
The Swan he has a bosom fair,
　And who so proud as he ?

Oh, yes, the Peacock is more proud
　Because his tail has eyes ;
The Lion roars so very loud,
　He'd fill you with surprise.

H

The Raven's coat is shining black,
   Or, rather, raven-grey ;
The Camel's bunch is on his back,
   The Owl abhors the day.

The Sparrow steals the cherry ripe,
   The Elephant is wise,
The Blackbird charms you with his pipe,
   The false Hyena cries.
The Hen guards well her little chicks,
   The Cow—her hoof is slit,
The Beaver builds with mud and sticks,
   The Lapwing cries " Peewit."

The little Wren is very small,
   The Humming-bird is less ;
The Lady-bird is least of all,
   And beautiful in dress.
The Pelican she loves her young,
   The Stork its parent loves,
The Woodcock's bill is very long,
   And innocent are Doves.

The streakèd Tiger's fond of blood,
   The Pigeon feeds on peas,
The Duck will gobble in the mud,
   The Mice will eat your cheese.
A Lobster's black, when boiled he's red,
   The harmless Lamb must bleed,
The Cod-fish has a clumsy head,
   The Goose on grass will feed.

The lady in her gown of silk
  The little Worm may thank;
The sick man drinks the Ass's milk,
  The Weasel's long and lank.
The Buck gives us a venison dish,
  When hunted for the spoil;
The Shark eats up the little fish,
  The Whale produces oil.

The Glow-worm shines the darkest night,
  With lantern in his tail;
The Turtle is the cit's delight,
  And wears a coat of mail.
In Germany they hunt the Boar,
  The Bee brings honey home,
The Ant lays up a winter store,
  The Bear loves honey-comb.

The Eagle has a crooked beak,
  The Plaice has orange spots,
The Starling, if he's taught, will speak;
  The Ostrich walks and trots.
The child that does not these things know
  Might well be called a dunce;
But I in knowledge quick will grow,
  For youth can come but once.

Ann and Jane Taylor.

Kindness to Animals

LITTLE children, never give
    Pain to things that feel and live:
Let the gentle robin come
For the crumbs you save at home,—
As his meat you throw along
He'll repay you with a song;
Never hurt the timid hare
Peeping from her green grass lair,
Let her come and sport and play
On the lawn at close of day;
The little lark goes soaring high
To the bright windows of the sky,
Singing as if 'twere always spring,
And fluttering on an untired wing,—
Oh! let him sing his happy song,
Nor do these gentle creatures wrong.

Anon.

UNNATURAL HISTORY

The Spider and the Fly   ❧   ❧   ❧   ❧

"WILL you walk into my parlour?" said the Spider
       to the Fly,
"'Tis the prettiest little parlour that ever you did spy;
The way into my parlour is up a winding stair,
And I have many curious things to show when you are
       there."
"Oh no, no," said the little Fly, "to ask me is in vain;
For who goes up your winding stair can ne'er come down
       again."

"I'm sure you must be weary, dear, with soaring up so high;
Will you rest upon my little bed?" said the Spider to the
       Fly.
"There are pretty curtains drawn around, the sheets are
       fine and thin;
And if you like to rest a while, I'll snugly tuck you in!"
"Oh no, no," said the little Fly, "for I've often heard it
       said,
They never, never wake again, who sleep upon your bed!"

Said the cunning Spider to the Fly, "Dear friend, what can
       I do
To prove the warm affection I've always felt for you?

I have, within my pantry, good store of all that's nice;
I'm sure you're very welcome—will you please to take a
slice?"
"Oh no, no," said the little Fly, "kind sir, that cannot be,
I've heard what's in your pantry, and I do not wish to see!"

"Sweet creature," said the Spider, "you're witty and you're
wise;
How handsome are your gauzy wings, how brilliant are your
eyes!
I have a little looking-glass upon my parlour shelf;
If you'll step in one moment, dear, you shall behold your-
self."
"I thank you, gentle sir," she said, "for what you're pleased
to say,
And bidding you good morning now, I'll call another day."

The Spider turned him round about, and went into his den,
For well he knew the silly Fly would soon be back again;
So he wove a subtle web in a little corner sly,
And set his table ready to dine upon the Fly.
Then he came out to his door again, and merrily did sing,—
"Come hither, hither, pretty Fly, with the pearl and silver
wing;
Your robes are green and purple, there's a crest upon your
head;
Your eyes are like the diamond bright, but mine are dull as
lead."

Alas, alas! how very soon this silly little Fly,
Hearing his wily, flattering words, came slowly flitting by:
With buzzing wings she hung aloft, then near and nearer
drew,—

Thinking only of her brilliant eyes, and green and purple
    hue ;
Thinking only of her crested head—poor foolish thing ! At
    last,
Up jumped the cunning Spider, and fiercely held her fast.
He dragged her up his winding stair, into his dismal den
Within his little parlour—but she ne'er came out again ! *

Mary Howitt.

The Cats' Tea-Party   ❧   ❧   ❧   ❧

FIVE little pussy-cats, invited out to tea,
    Cried : " Mother, let us go—Oh, do ! for good we'll
    surely be.
We'll wear our bibs and hold our things as you have shown
    us how—
Spoons in right paws, cups in left—and make a pretty bow ;
We'll always say ' Yes, if you please,' and ' Only half of
    that.' "
" Then go, my darling children," said the happy Mother
    Cat.
The five little pussy-cats went out that night to tea,
Their heads were smooth and glossy, their tails were swing-
    ing free ;
They held their things as they had learned, and tried to be
    polite ;—
With snowy bibs beneath their chins they were a pretty
    sight.
But, alas, for manners beautiful, and coats as soft as silk !
The moment that the little kits were asked to take some
    milk,

* Four lines of advice omitted.

They dropped their spoons, forgot to bow, and—oh, what
    do you think?
They put their noses in the cups and all began to drink!
Yes, every naughty little kit set up a miou for more,
Then knocked the tea-cups over, and scampered through
    the door.

                                       F. E. Weatherley.

Pussy-Cat ∽ ∽ ∽ ∽ ∽ ∽

PUSSY-CAT lives in the servants' hall,
    She can set up her back, and purr;
The little Mice live in a crack in the wall,
    But they hardly dare venture to stir;

For whenever they think of taking the air,
    Or filling their little maws,
The Pussy-Cat says, "Come out, if you dare;
    I will catch you all with my claws."

Scrabble, scrabble, scrabble, went all the little Mice,
    For they smelt the Cheshire cheese;
The Pussy-Cat said, "It smells very nice,
    Now *do* come out, if you please."

"Squeak," said the little Mouse; "Squeak, squeak, squeak,"
    Said all the young ones too;
"We never creep out when cats are about,
    Because we're afraid of *you.*"

So the cunning old Cat lay down on a mat
  By the fire in the servants' hall ;
" If the little Mice peep, they'll think I'm asleep ";
  So she rolled herself up like a ball.

" Squeak," said the little Mouse, " we'll creep out
  And eat some Cheshire cheese,
That silly old Cat is asleep on the mat,
  And we may sup at our ease."

Nibble, nibble, nibble, went all the little Mice,
  And they licked their little paws ;
Then the cunning old Cat sprang up from the mat,
  And caught them all with her claws.

  " Aunt Effie."

The Last Dying Speech and Confession of Poor Puss ∾ ∾ ∾ ∾ ∾

" KIND masters and misses, whoever you be,
    Do stop for a moment and pity poor me !
While here on my death-bed I try to relate
My many misfortunes and miseries great.

My dear Mother Tabby I've often heard say,
That I *have* been a very fine cat in my day ;
But the sorrows in which my whole life has been passed
Have spoiled all my beauty, and killed me at last.

Poor thoughtless young thing ! if I recollect right,
I was kittened in March, on a clear frosty night ;
And before I could see, or was half a week old,
I nearly had perished, the barn was so cold.

But this chilly spring I got pretty well over,
And moused in the hay-loft, or played in the clover,
Or till I was weary, which seldom occurred,
Ran after my tail, which I took for a bird.

But, ah ! my poor tail, and my pretty sleek ears !
The farmer's boy cut them all off with his shears :
How little I thought, when I licked them so clean,
I should be such a figure, not fit to be seen !

Some time after this, when the places were healed,
As I lay in the sun, sound asleep in the field,
Miss Fanny crept slyly, and gripping me fast,
Declared she had caught the sweet creature at last.

Ah me ! how I struggled my freedom to gain,
But, alas ! all my kicking and struggles were vain,
For she held me so tight in her pinafore tied,
That before she got home I had like to have died.

From this dreadful morning my sorrows arose !
Wherever I went I was followed with blows :
Some kicked me for nothing while quietly sleeping,
Or flogged me for daring the pantry to peep in.

And then the great dog ! I shall never forget him ;
How many a time my young master would set him,
And while I stood terrified, all of a quake,
Cry, 'Hey, cat !' and 'Seize her, boy ! give her a shake !'

Sometimes, when so hungry I could not forbear
Just taking a scrap, that I thought they could spare,
Oh ! what have I suffered with beating and banging,
Or starved for a fortnight, or threatened with hanging.

But kicking, and beating, and starving, and that,
I have borne with the spirit becoming a cat :
There was but one thing which I could not sustain,
So great was my sorrow, so hopeless my pain :—

One morning, laid safe in a warm little bed,
That down in the stable I'd carefully spread,
Three sweet little kittens as ever you saw,
I hid, as I thought, in some trusses of straw.

I was never so happy, I think, nor so proud,
I mewed to my kittens, and purred out aloud,
And thought with delight of the merry carousing
We'd have, when I first took them with me a-mousing.

But how shall I tell you the sorrowful ditty ?
I'm sure it would melt even Growler to pity ;
For the very next morning my darlings I found
Lying dead by the horse-pond, all mangled and drowned.

Poor darlings, I dragged them along to the stable,
And did all to warm them a mother was able ;
But, alas ! all my licking and mewing were vain,
And I thought I should never be happy again.

However, time gave me a little relief,
And mousing diverted the thoughts of my grief ;
And at last I began to be gay and content,
Till one dreadful night I sincerely repent.

Miss Fanny was fond of a little canary,
That tempted me more than mouse, pantry, or dairy;
So, not having eaten a morsel all day,
I flew to the bird-cage, and tore it away.

Now tell me, my friends, was the like ever heard,
That a cat should be killed for just catching a bird!
And I'm sure not the slightest suspicion I had,
But that catching a mouse was exactly as bad.

Indeed I can say, with my paw on my heart,
I would not have acted a mischievous part;
But, as dear Mother Tabby was often repeating,
I thought birds and mice were on purpose for eating.

Be this as it may, when my supper was o'er,
And but a few feathers were left on the floor,
Came Fanny—and scolding, and fighting, and crying,
She gave me those bruises, of which I am dying.

But I feel that my breathing grows shorter apace,
And cold clammy sweats trickle down from my face:
I forgive little Fanny this bruise on my side—"
She stopped, gave a sigh, and a struggle, and died!

Ann and Jane Taylor.

The Three Little Pigs

A JOLLY old sow once lived in a sty,
And three little piggies had she;
And she waddled about, saying, "Umph! umph! umph!"
While the little ones said, "Wee! wee!"

"My dear little brothers," said one of the brats,
    "My dear little piggies," said he;
"Let us all for the future say, 'Umph! umph! umph!'
    'Tis so childish to say, 'Wee! wee!'"

Then these little pigs grew skinny and lean,
    And lean they might very well be;
For somehow they *couldn't* say, "Umph! umph! umph!"
    And they *wouldn't* say, "Wee! wee! wee!"

So after a time these little pigs died,
    They all died of *felo de se;*
From trying too hard to say, "Umph! umph! umph!"
    When they only could say, "Wee! wee!"

Moral

A moral there is to this little song,
    A moral that's easy to see;
Don't try while yet young to say, "Umph! umph! umph!"
    For you only can say, "Wee! wee!"
                                        A. S. Scott-Gatty.

Dame Duck's First Lecture on Education   ⌒

OLD Mother Duck has hatched a brood
    Of ducklings, small and callow;
Their little wings are short, their down
    Is mottled gray and yellow.

There is a quiet little stream,
   That runs into the moat,
Where tall green sedges spread their leaves,
   And water-lilies float.

Close by the margin of the brook
   The old duck made her nest,
Of straw, and leaves, and withered grass,
   And down from her own breast.

And then she sat for four long weeks
   In rainy days and fine,
Until the ducklings all came out—
   Four, five, six, seven, eight, nine.

One peeped out from beneath her wing,
   One scrambled on her back ;
" That's very rude," said old Dame Duck,
   " Get off! quack, quack, quack, quack ! "

" 'Tis close," said Dame Duck, shoving out
   The egg-shells with her bill ;
" Besides, it never suits young ducks
   To keep them sitting still."

So, rising from her nest, she said,
   " Now, children, look at me ;
A well-bred duck should waddle so,
   From side to side—d'ye see ? "

" Yes," said the little ones, and then
   She went on to explain :
" A well-bred duck turns in its toes
   As I do—try again."

"Yes," said the ducklings, waddling on :
 "That's better," said their mother ;
"But well-bred ducks walk in a row,
 Straight—one behind another."

"Yes," said the little ducks again,
 All waddling in a row :
"Now to the pond," said old Dame Duck—
 Splash, splash, and in they go.

"Let me swim first," said old Dame Duck,
 "To this side, now to that ;
There, snap at those great brown-winged flies,
 They make young ducklings fat.

"Now when you reach the poultry-yard,
 The hen-wife, Molly Head,
Will feed you, with the other fowls,
 On bran and mashed-up bread.

"The hens will peck and fight, but mind,
 I hope that all of you
Will gobble up the food as fast
 As well-bred ducks should do.

"You'd better get into the dish,
 Unless it is too small ;
In that case, I should use my foot,
 And overturn it all."

The ducklings did as they were bid,
 And found the plan so good,
That, from that day, the other fowls
 Got hardly any food.

         "Aunt Effie."

The Notorious Glutton ∿ ∿ ∿

A DUCK who had got such a habit of stuffing,
    That all the day long she was panting and puffing,
And by every creature who did her great crop see,
Was thought to be galloping fast for a dropsy;

One day, after eating a plentiful dinner,
With full twice as much as there should have been in her,
While up to her forehead still greedily roking,
Was greatly alarmed by the symptoms of choking.

Now there was an old fellow, much famed for discerning
(A drake, who had taken a liking for learning),
And high in repute with his feathery friends,
Was called Dr. Drake: for this doctor she sends.

In a hole of the dunghill was Dr. Drake's shop,
Where he kept a few simples for curing the crop;
Small pebbles, and two or three different gravels,
With certain famed plants he had found in his travels.

So taking a handful of suitable things,
And brushing his topple and pluming his wings,
And putting his feathers in apple-pie order,
He went to prescribe for the lady's disorder.

"Dear sir," said the duck, with a delicate quack,
Just turning a little way round on her back,
And leaning her head on a stone in the yard,
"My case, Dr. Drake, is exceedingly hard.

"I feel so distended with wind, and opprest,
So squeamish and faint, such a load at my chest;
And, day after day, I assure you it *is* hard,
To suffer with patience these pains in my gizzard."

"Give me leave," said the doctor with medical look,
As her cold flabby paw in his fingers he took;
"By the feel of your pulse, your complaint, I've been thinking,
Must surely be owing to eating and drinking."

"Oh! no, sir, believe me," the lady replied
(Alarmed for her stomach, as well as her pride),
"I'm sure it arises from nothing I eat,
But I rather suspect I got wet in my feet.

"I've only been raking a bit in the gutter,
Where cook has been pouring some cold melted butter,
And a slice of green cabbage, and scraps of cold meat:
Just a trifle or two, that I thought I could eat."

The doctor was just to his business proceeding,
By gentle emetics, a blister, and bleeding,
When all on a sudden she rolled on her side,
Gave a terrible quack, and a struggle, and died!

Her remains were interred in a neighbouring swamp
By her friends with a great deal of funeral pomp;
But I've heard, this inscription her tombstone displayed:
"Here poor Mrs. Duck, the great glutton, is laid";
And all the young ducklings are brought by their friends
There to learn the disgrace in which gluttony ends.

Ann and Jane Taylor.

The Butterfly's Ball ∽ ∽ ∽ ∽

" COME, take up your hats, and away let us haste
        To the Butterfly's Ball and the Grasshopper's Feast,
The Trumpeter, Gadfly, has summon'd the crew,
And the Revels are now only waiting for you."

So said little Robert, and pacing along,
His merry Companions came forth in a throng,
And on the smooth Grass by the side of a Wood,
Beneath a broad oak that for ages had stood,
Saw the Children of Earth and the Tenants of Air
For an Evening's Amusement together repair.

And there came the Beetle, so blind and so black,
Who carried the Emmet, his friend, on his back.
And there was the Gnat and the Dragon-fly too,
With all their Relations, green, orange and blue.
And there came the Moth, with his plumage of down,
And the Hornet in jacket of yellow and brown;
Who with him the Wasp, his companion, did bring,
But they promised that evening to lay by their sting.
And the sly little Dormouse crept out of his hole,
And brought to the Feast his blind Brother, the Mole.
And the Snail, with his horns peeping out of his shell,
Came from a great distance, the length of an ell.

A Mushroom their Table, and on it was laid
A water-dock leaf, which a table-cloth made.
The Viands were various, to each of their taste,
And the Bee brought her honey to crown the Repast.
Then close on his haunches, so solemn and wise,
The Frog from a corner look'd up to the skies;

And the Squirrel, well pleased such diversions to see,
Mounted high overhead and look'd down from a tree.

Then out came the Spider, with finger so fine,
To show his dexterity on the tight-line.
From one branch to another, his cobwebs he slung,
Then quick as an arrow he darted along,
But just in the middle—oh! shocking to tell,
From his rope, in an instant, poor Harlequin fell.
Yet he touch'd not the ground, but with talons outspread,
Hung suspended in air, at the end of a thread.

Then the Grasshopper came with a jerk and a spring,
Very long was his Leg, though but short was his Wing;
He took but three leaps, and was soon out of sight,
Then chirp'd his own praises the rest of the night.
With step so majestic the Snail did advance,
And promised the Gazers a Minuet to dance;
But they all laughed so loud that he pulled in his head,
And went in his own little chamber to bed.
Then as Evening gave way to the shadows of Night,
Their Watchman, the Glowworm, came out with a light.

"Then Home let us hasten, while yet we can see,
For no Watchman is waiting for you and for me."
So said little Robert, and pacing along,
His merry Companions return'd in a throng.

                                        T. Roscoe.

The Owl-Critic ∽ ∽ ∽ ∽ ∽

"WHO stuffed that white owl?" No one spoke in the
        shop:
The barber was busy, and he couldn't stop;
The customers, waiting their turns, were all reading
The *Daily*, the *Herald*, the *Post*, little heeding
The young man who blurted out such a blunt question;
Not one raised a head, or even made a suggestion;
        And the barber kept on shaving.

"Don't you see, Mister Brown,"
Cried the youth, with a frown,
"How wrong the whole thing is,
How preposterous each wing is,
How flattened the head is, how jammed down the neck is—
In short, the whole owl, what an ignorant wreck 'tis!
I make no apology;
I've learned owl-eology.
I've passed days and nights in a hundred collections,
And cannot be blinded to any deflections
Arising from unskilful fingers that fail
To stuff a bird right, from his beak to his tail.
Mister Brown! Mister Brown!
Do take that bird down,
Or you'll soon be the laughing-stock all over town!"
        And the barber kept on shaving.

"I've *studied* owls
And other night fowls,
And I tell you
What I know to be true:
An owl cannot roost
With his limbs so unloosed;

No owl in this world
Ever had his claws curled,
Ever had his legs slanted,
Ever had his bill canted,
Ever had his neck screwed
Into that attitude.
He can't *do* it, because
'Tis against all bird-laws.
Anatomy teaches,
Ornithology preaches
An owl has a toe
That *can't* turn out so!
I've made the white owl my study for years,
And to see such a job almost moves me to tears!
Mister Brown, I'm amazed
You should be so gone crazed
As to put up a bird
In that posture absurd!
To *look* at that owl really brings on a dizziness;
The man who stuffed *him* don't half know his business!"
   And the barber kept on shaving.

"Examine those eyes.
I'm filled with surprise
Taxidermists should pass
Off on you such poor glass;
So unnatural they seem
They'd make Audubon scream,
And John Burroughs laugh
To encounter such chaff.
Do take that bird down;
Have him stuffed again, Brown!"
   And the barber kept on shaving.

" With some sawdust and bark
I could stuff in the dark
An owl better than that.
I could make an old hat
Look more like an owl
Than that horrid fowl,
Stuck up there so stiff like a side of coarse leather.
In fact, about *him* there's not one natural feather."

Just then, with a wink and a sly normal lurch,
The owl, very gravely, got down from his perch,
Walked round, and regarded his fault-finding critic
(Who thought he was stuffed) with a glance analytic,
And then fairly hooted, as if he should say:
" Your learning's at fault *this* time, any way;
Don't waste it again on a live bird, I pray.
I'm an owl; you're another.   Sir Critic, good-day!"
   And the barber kept on shaving.
        James T. Fields.

POETS AT PLAY

Jemima ❧ ❧ ❧

THERE was a little girl, she wore a little hood,
    And a curl down the middle of her forehead,
When she was good, she was very, very good,
    But when she was bad, she was horrid.

One day she went upstairs, while her parents, unawares,
    In the kitchen down below were occupied with meals,
And she stood upon her head, on her little truckle-bed,
    And she then began hurraying with her heels.

Her mother heard the noise, and thought it was the boys,
    A-playing at a combat in the attic,
But when she climbed the stair and saw Jemima there,
    She took and she did whip her most emphatic !

Anon.

A Strange Wild Song ❧

HE thought he saw a Buffalo
    Upon the chimney-piece:
He looked again, and found it was
    His Sister's Husband's Niece.
"Unless you leave this house," he said,
    "I'll send for the Police."

He thought he saw a Rattlesnake
    That questioned him in Greek :
He looked again, and found it was
    The Middle of Next Week.
"The one thing I regret," he said,
    "Is that it cannot speak ! "

He thought he saw a Banker's Clerk
    Descending from the 'bus :
He looked again, and found it was
    A Hippopotamus.
"If this should stay to dine," he said,
    "There won't be much for us ! "

He thought he saw a Kangaroo
    That worked a coffee-mill :
He looked again, and found it was
    A Vegetable-Pill.
"Were I to swallow this," he said,
    "I should be very ill."

He thought he saw a Coach and Four
    That stood beside his bed :
He looked again and found it was
    A Bear without a Head.
"Poor thing," he said, "poor silly thing !
    It's waiting to be fed ! "

He thought he saw an Albatross
    That fluttered round the Lamp :
He looked again, and found it was
    A Penny Postage-Stamp.
"You'd best be getting home," he said :
    "The nights are very damp ! "

He thought he saw a Garden Door
   That opened with a key :
He looked again, and found it was
   A Double-Rule-of-Three :
" And all its mystery," he said,
   " Is clear as day to me ! "

He thought he saw an Argument
   That proved he was the Pope :
He looked again, and found it was
   A Bar of Mottled Soap.
" A fact so dread," he faintly said,
   " Extinguishes all hope ! "

Lewis Carroll.

Sage Counsel   ∽   ∽   ∽

THE lion is the beast to fight :
   He leaps along the plain,
And if you run with all your might,
   He runs with all his mane.
      I'm glad I'm not a Hottentot,
      But if I were, with outward cal-lum
      I'd either faint upon the spot
      Or hie me up a leafy pal-lum.

The chamois is the beast to hunt :
   He's fleeter than the wind,
And when the chamois is in front
   The hunter is behind.

The Tyrolese make famous cheese
And hunt the chamois o'er the chaz-zums ;
I'd choose the former, if you please,
For precipices give me spaz-zums.

The polar bear will make a rug
  Almost as white as snow :
But if he gets you in his hug,
  He rarely lets you go.
    And Polar ice looks very nice,
    With all the colours of a prissum :
    But, if you'll follow my advice,
    Stay home and learn your catechissum.

A. T. Q. C.

The Elephant ∾ ∾ ∾ ∾

WHEN people call this beast to mind,
  They marvel more and more
At such a LITTLE tail behind,
  So LARGE a trunk before.

Hilaire Belloc.

The Lion ∾ ∾ ∾ ∾ ∾

THE Lion, the Lion, he dwells in the waste,
  He has a big head and a very small waist ;
But his shoulders are stark, and his jaws they are grim,
And a good little child will not play with him.

Hilaire Belloc.

The Frog ∾ ∾ ∾

BE kind and tender to the Frog,
  And do not call him names,
As "Slimy-skin," or "Polly-wog,"
  Or likewise "Uncle James,"
Or "Gape-a-grin," or "Toad-gone-wrong,"
  Or " Billy Bandy-knees ":
The Frog is justly sensitive
  To epithets like these.

No animal will more repay
  A treatment kind and fair,
At least so lonely people say
Who keep a frog (and, by the way,
  They are extremely rare).

Hilaire Belloc.

Ode to a Rhinoceros ∾ ∾

RHINOCEROS, your hide looks all undone,
  You do not take my fancy in the least :
You have a horn where other brutes have none :
  Rhinoceros, you are an ugly beast.

Hilaire Belloc.

An Elegy on the Death of a Mad Dog   ∾

GOOD people all, of every sort,
   Give ear unto my song;
And if you find it wondrous short,—
   It cannot hold you long.

In Islington there was a man,
   Of whom the world might say,
That still a godly race he ran,—
   Whene'er he went to pray.

A kind and gentle heart he had,
   To comfort friends and foes;
The naked every day he clad,—
   When he put on his clothes.

And in that town a dog was found,
   As many dogs there be,
Both mongrel, puppy, whelp and hound,
   And curs of low degree.

This dog and man at first were friends;
   But when a pique began,
The dog, to gain some private ends,
   Went mad, and bit the man.

Around from all the neighbouring streets
   The wondering neighbours ran,
And swore the dog had lost his wits,
   To bite so good a man.

The wound it seem'd both sore and sad
   To every Christian eye:

And while they swore the dog was mad,
   They swore the man would die.

But soon a wonder came to light,
   That show'd the rogues they lied ;
The man recover'd of the bite,
   The dog it was that died.

           Oliver Goldsmith.

History ～ ～ ～ ～ ～

WHEN good King Arthur ruled this land,
   He was a goodly king ;
He stole three pecks of barley meal,
   To make a bag-pudding.

A bag-pudding the king did make,
   And stuff'd it well with plums :
And in it put great lumps of fat,
   As big as my two thumbs.

The king and queen did eat thereof,
   And noblemen beside ;
And what they could not eat that night,
   The queen next morning fried.

           Old Rhyme.

The Walrus and the Carpenter ◡

THE sun was shining on the sea,
  Shining with all his might:
He did his very best to make
  The billows smooth and bright—
And this was odd, because it was
  The middle of the night.

The moon was shining sulkily,
  Because she thought the sun
Had got no business to be there
  After the day was done—
"It's very rude of him," she said,
  "To come and spoil the fun!"

The sea was wet as wet could be,
  The sands were dry as dry.
You could not see a cloud, because
  No cloud was in the sky:
No birds were flying overhead—
  There were no birds to fly.

The Walrus and the Carpenter
  Were walking close at hand;
They wept like anything to see
  Such quantities of sand:
"If this were only cleared away,"
  They said, "it *would* be grand!"

"If seven maids with seven mops
  Swept it for half a year,

Do you suppose," the Walrus said,
    "That they could get it clear?"
" I doubt it," said the Carpenter,
    And shed a bitter tear.

" O Oysters, come and walk with us!"
    The Walrus did beseech.
' A pleasant walk, a pleasant talk,
    Along the briny beach :
We cannot do with more than four,
    To give a hand to each."

The eldest Oyster looked at him,
    But never a word he said :
The eldest Oyster winked his eye,
    And shook his heavy head—
Meaning to say he did not choose
    To leave the oyster-bed.

But four young Oysters hurried up,
    All eager for the treat :
Their coats were brushed, their faces washed
    Their shoes were clean and neat—
And this was odd, because, you know,
    They hadn't any feet.

Four other Oysters followed them,
    And yet another four ;
And thick and fast they came at last,
    And more, and more, and more—
All hopping through the frothy waves,
    And scrambling to the shore.

The Walrus and the Carpenter
   Walked on a mile or so,
And then they rested on a rock
   Conveniently low :
And all the little Oysters stood
   And waited in a row.

" The time has come," the Walrus said,
   " To talk of many things :
Of shoes—and ships—and sealing-wax—
   Of cabbages—and kings—
And why the sea is boiling hot—
   And whether pigs have wings."

" But, wait a bit," the Oysters cried,
   " Before we have our chat ;
For some of us are out of breath,
   And all of us are fat !"
" No hurry !" said the Carpenter.
   They thanked him much for that.

" A loaf of bread," the Walrus said,
   " Is what we chiefly need :
Pepper and vinegar besides
   Are very good indeed—
Now if you're ready, Oysters dear,
   We can begin to feed."

" But not on us !" the Oysters cried,
   Turning a little blue.
" After such kindness, that would be
   A dismal thing to do !"
" The night is fine," the Walrus said.
   " Do you admire the view ?

"It was so kind of you to come!
  And you are very nice!"
The Carpenter said nothing but
  "Cut me another slice:
I wish you were not quite so deaf—
  I've had to ask you twice!"

"It seems a shame," the Walrus said,
  "To play them such a trick,
After we've brought them out so far,
  And made them trot so quick!'
The Carpenter said nothing but
  "The butter's spread too thick!"

"I weep for you," the Walrus said:
  "I deeply sympathise."
With sobs and tears he sorted out
  Those of the largest size,
Holding his pocket-handkerchief
  Before his streaming eyes.

"O Oysters," said the Carpenter,
  "You've had a pleasant run!
Shall we be trotting home again?"
  But answer came there none—
And this was scarcely odd, because
  They'd eaten every one.

Lewis Carroll.

The Pobble Who Has No Toes ∽ ∽

I

THE Pobble who has no toes
   Had once as many as we;
When they said, " Some day you may lose them all ";
   He replied—" Fish fiddle-de-dee ! "
And his Aunt Jobiska made him drink
Lavender water tinged with pink,
For she said, " The World in general knows
There's nothing so good for a Pobble's toes ! "

II

The Pobble who has no toes
   Swam across the Bristol Channel;
But before he set out he wrapped his nose
   In a piece of scarlet flannel.
For his Aunt Jobiska said, " No harm
Can come to his toes if his nose is warm ;
And it's perfectly known that a Pobble's toes
Are safe,—provided he minds his nose."

III

The Pobble swam fast and well,
   And when boats or ships came near him,
He tinkledy-binkledy-winkled a bell,
   So that all the world could hear him.
And all the Sailors and Admirals cried,
When they saw him nearing the further side,—
" He has gone to fish, for his Aunt Jobiska's
Runcible Cat with crimson whiskers ! "

IV

But before he touched the shore,
   The shore of the Bristol Channel,
A sea-green Porpoise carried away
   His wrapper of scarlet flannel.
And when he came to observe his feet,
Formerly garnished with toes so neat,
His face at once became forlorn
On perceiving that all his toes were gone !

V

And nobody ever knew,
   From that dark day to the present,
Whoso had taken the Pobble's toes,
   In a manner so far from pleasant.
Whether the shrimps or crawfish gray,
Or crafty mermaids stole them away—
Nobody knew ; and nobody knows
How the Pobble was robbed of his twice five toes !

VI

The Pobble who has no toes
   Was placed in a friendly Bark,
And they rowed him back, and carried him up
   To his Aunt Jobiska's Park.
And she made him a feast at his earnest wish
Of eggs and buttercups fried with fish ;—
And she said,—" It's a fact the whole world knows,
That Pobbles are happier without their toes."

Edward Lear.

The Author of the " Pobble " ⌒

H OW pleasant to know Mr. Lear!
  Who has written such volumes of stuff!
Some think him ill-tempered and queer,
  But a few think him pleasant enough.

His mind is concrete and fastidious,
  His nose is remarkably big;
His visage is more or less hideous,
  His beard it resembles a wig.

He has ears, and two eyes, and ten fingers,
  Leastways if you reckon two thumbs ,
Long ago he was one of the singers,
  But now he is one of the dumbs.

He sits in a beautiful parlour,
  With hundreds of books on the wall;
He drinks a great deal of Marsala,
  But never gets tipsy at all.

He has many friends, laymen and clerical,
  Old Foss is the name of his cat:
His body is perfectly spherical,
  He weareth a runcible hat.

When he walks in a waterproof white,
  The children run after him so!
Calling out, " He's come out in his night-
  gown, that crazy old Englishman, oh! "

He weeps by the side of the ocean,
　　He weeps on the top of the hill;
He purchases pancakes and lotion,
　　And chocolate shrimps from the mill.

He reads but he cannot speak Spanish,
　　He cannot abide ginger-beer:
Ere the days of his pilgrimage vanish,
　　How pleasant to know Mr. Lear!

　　　　　　　　　　　　　　　Edward Lear.

The Story of Little Suck-a-Thumb

ONE day, mamma said: "Conrad dear,
　　I must go out and leave you here.
But mind now, Conrad, what I say,
Don't suck your thumb while I'm away.
The great tall tailor always comes
To little boys that suck their thumbs;
And ere they dream what he's about,
He takes his great sharp scissors out
And cuts their thumbs clean off,—and then,
You know, they never grow again."

Mamma had scarcely turned her back,
The thumb was in, alack! alack!
The door flew open, in he ran,
The great, long, red-legged scissor-man.
Oh, children, see! the tailor's come
And caught our little Suck-a-Thumb.
Snip! snap! snip! the scissors go;
And Conrad cries out—"Oh! oh! oh!"

Snip! snap! snip!   They go so fast,
That both his thumbs are off at last.

Mamma comes home; there Conrad stands,
And looks quite sad, and shows his hands;—
"Ah!" said mamma, "I knew he'd come
To naughty little Suck-a-Thumb."

Dr. Heinrich Hoffmann (translated).

The Sad Story of a Little Boy that Cried   ∽

ONCE a little boy, Jack, was, oh! ever so good,
    Till he took a strange notion to cry all he could.

So he cried all the day, and he cried all the night,
He cried in the morning and in the twilight;

He cried till his voice was as hoarse as a crow,
And his mouth grew so large it looked like a great O.

It grew at the bottom, and grew at the top;
It grew till they thought that it never would stop.

Each day his great mouth grew taller and taller,
And his dear little self grew smaller and smaller.

At last, that same mouth grew so big that—alack!—
It was only a mouth with a border of Jack.*

From " St. Nicholas."

* Two lines omitted.

The Man in the Moon ∽ ∽ ∽

SAID the Raggedy Man on a hot afternoon,
 "My!
        Sakes!
            What a lot o' mistakes
Some little folks makes on The Man in the Moon!
But people that's b'en up to *see* him, like *me*,
And calls on him frequent and intimutly,
Might drop a few hints that would interest you
        Clean!
            Through!—
                If you wanted 'em to—
Some *actual* facts that might interest you!

O The Man in the Moon has a crick in his back;
        Whee!
            Whimm!
                Ain't you sorry for him?
And a mole on his nose that is purple and black;
And his eyes are so weak that they water and run
If he dares to *dream* even he looks at the sun,—
So he jes' dreams of stars, as the doctors advise—
        My!
            Eyes!
                But isn't he wise—
To jes' dream of stars, as the doctors advise?

And The Man in the Moon has a boil on his ear—
        Whee!
            Whing!
                What a singular thing!
I know! but these facts are authentic, my dear,—
There's a boil on his ear; and a corn on his chin,—

He calls it a dimple—but dimples stick in—
Yet it might be a dimple turned over, you know!
>Whang!
>>Ho!
>>>Why, certainly so!—
It might be a dimple turned over, you know!

And The Man in the Moon has a rheumatic knee,
>Gee!
>>Whizz!
>>>What a pity that is!
And his toes have worked round where his heels ought to be.
So whenever he wants to go North he goes *South*,
And comes back with porridge crumbs all round his mouth,
And he brushes them off with a Japanese fan.
>Whing!
>>Whann!
>>>What a marvellous man!
What a very remarkably marvellous man!

And The Man in the Moon," sighed the Raggedy Man
>"Gits!
>>So!
>>>Sullonesome, you know,—
Up there by hisse'f sence creation began!—
That when I call on him and then come away,
He grabs me and holds me and begs me to stay,—
Till—*Well* if it wasn't for *Jimmy-cum-Jim*,
>Dadd!
>>Limb!
>>>I'd go pardners with *him*—
Jes' jump my bob here and be pardners with him!"

James Whitcomb Riley.

A Warning   ∽   ∽   ∽

THREE children sliding on the ice
   Upon a summer's day,
It so fell out they all fell in,
   The rest they ran away.

Now had these children been at home,
   Or sliding on dry ground,
Ten thousand pounds to one penny
   They had not all been drown'd.

You parents all that children have,
   And you that have got none,
If you would have them safe abroad,
   Pray keep them safe at home.

John Gay.

An Unsuspected Fact   ∽

IF down his throat a man should choose
   In fun, to jump or slide,
He'd scrape his shoes against his teeth,
   Nor dirt his own inside.
But if his teeth were lost and gone,
And not a stump to scrape upon,
He'd see at once how very pat
His tongue lay there, by way of mat,
And he would wipe his feet on *that!*

Rev. Edward Cannon.

The Snuff-Boxes ∾ ∾ ∾ ∾

A VILLAGE pedagogue announced one day
    Unto his pupils, that Inspector A.
Was coming to examine them.   Quoth he :
" If he should try you in Geography,
Most likely he will ask—' What's the Earth's shape ? '
Then, if you feel as stupid as an ape,
Just look at me : my snuff-box I will show,
Which will remind you it is round, you know."

Now, the sagacious master, I declare,
Had two snuff-boxes—one round, t'other square ;
The square he carried through the week, the round
On Sundays only.
            Hark ! a footstep's sound :
'Tis the Inspector.   "What's the Earth's shape, lad ? "
Addressing one by name.   The latter, glad
To have his memory helped, looked at the master ;
When, piteous to relate, O, sad disaster !
The pupil without hesitation says :
" Round, sir, on Sundays, square on other days."

Anon.

Quite a History ∾ ∾ ∾ ∾

" WHERE have you been, Lysander Pratt ? "
      " In Greedy Land, Philander Sprat."
" What did you there to grow so fat ? "

" I built myself a little house
In which I lived snug as a mouse."

"Well, very, very good was that ! "
"Not wholly good, Philander Sprat."
"Now, wherefore not, Lysander Pratt ? "

" A bear came raging from the wood,
And tumbled down my cottage good."

" Alas ! how very bad was that ! "
" Not wholly bad, Philander Sprat."
" Not bad ?   Why not, Lysander Pratt ? "

" I killed the bear, and of his skin
I made a coat to wrap me in."

" Well done !   Now surely good was that ! "
" Yet not so good, Philander Sprat."
" Now, why not good, Lysander Pratt ?

" A wicked hound tore up my coat
Until it was not worth a groat."

" Ah, what an evil thing was that ! "
" Not wholly bad, Philander Sprat."
" What good was there, Lysander Pratt ? "

" He caught for me a great wild boar,
That made me sausages good store."

" What luck !   How very good was that ! "
" Good ?   Not all good, Philander Sprat."
" Why not all good, Lysander Pratt ? "

"A cat stole in on velvet paw,
And ate them all with greedy maw."

"Now surely wholly bad was that!"
"Not wholly bad, Philander Sprat."
"Then tell me why, Lysander Pratt."

"Of Pussy's fur with silken hair,
I made of gloves a noble pair."

"Trust you! No wonder you are fat!
You found your good account in that,
As in all else, Lysander Pratt."

"Yes, in the closet hang they now,
Yet they are full of holes, I vow,

Gnawed by some thievish long-tailed rat;
And so, you see, Philander Sprat,
Not wholly good was even that!"

Arlo Bates.

The Wreck of the Steamship "Puffin" ⌁ ⌁

TELL you a story, children? Well, gather around my
    knee,
And I'll see if I cannot thrill you (though you're torpid
    after your tea),
With a moving tale of a shipwreck; and—should you refrain
    from sleep,
For the cake was a trifle heavy—I flatter myself you'll weep!

You all know Kensington Gardens, and some of you, I'll
      be bound,
Have stood by the level margin of the Pond that's entitled
      "Round";
'Tis a pleasant spot on a summer day, when the air is laden
      with balm,
And the snowy sails are reflected clear in a mirror of flaw-
      less calm!

Well, it isn't like that in the winter, when the gardens are
      shut at four,
And a wind is lashing the water, and driving the ducks
      ashore.
Ah! the Pond can be black and cruel then, with its waves
      running inches high,
And a peril lurks for the tautest yacht that pocket-money
      can buy!

Yet, in weather like this, with a howling blast and a sky of
      ominous gloom,
Did the good ship *Puffin* put out to sea, as if trying to
      tempt her doom!
She was a model steamer, on the latest approved design,
And her powerful 10-slug engines were driven by spirits of
      wine.

And a smarter crew (they were sixpence each!) never
      shipped on a model bark,
While her Captain, "Nuremberg Noah," had once com-
      manded an ark;
Like a fine old salt of the olden school, he had stuck to his
      wooden ship,
But lately, he'd been promoted—and this was his trial trip.

Off went the *Puffin* when steam was up, with her crew and
    commander brave !
And her screw was whizzing behind her as she breasted
    the foaming wave ;
Danger? each sixpenny seaman smiled at the notion of that!
But the face of the skipper looked thoughtful from under
    his broad-brimmed hat.

Was he thinking of his children three—of Japheth, and
    Ham, and Shem ?
Or his elephants (both with a trunk unglued !), was he sad
    at the thought of them ?
Or the door at the end of his own old ark—did it give him
    a passing pain
To reflect that its unreal knocker might never deceive him
    again ?

Nay, children, I cannot answer—he had passed inquiry
    beyond :
He was far away on the billowy waste of the wild and heav-
    ing Pond,
Battling hard with the angry crests of the waves, that were
    rolling in
And seeking to overwhelm and swamp his staggering
    vessel of tin !

Suddenly, speed she slackened, and seemed of her task to
    tire . . .
Aye ! for the seas she had shipped of late had extinguished
    her engine fire !
And the park-keeper, watching her, shook his head and in
    manner unfeeling cried :
" 'Twill be nothing short of a miracle now if she makes the
    opposite side ! "

Think of it, children—that tiny ship, tossed in the boiling
    froth,
Drifting about at the wild caprice of the elements' fitful
    wrath !
Her screw-propeller was useless now that the flickering
    flame was out,
And the invalids gazed from their snug bath chairs, till they
    almost forgot the gout.

Help for the gallant vessel ! she is overborne by the blast !
She is shipping water by spoonfuls now, I tell you she's
    sinking fast !
" Hi ! " cried one of her owners to a spaniel, liver and
    black,
" Good dog, into the water quick ! " . . . But the park-
    keeper held it back !

Yes, spite of indignant pleadings from the eager excited
    crowd,
He quoted a pedant bye-law : " In the water no dogs
    allowed."
Then shame on the regulations that would hinder an honest
    dog
From plunging in to assist a ship that is rolling a helpless
    log !

Stand by all ! for she'll ride it out—though she's left to do
    it alone.
She was drifting in, she was close at hand—when down she
    went like a stone !
A few feet more and they had her safe—and now, it was all
    too late,
For the *Puffin* had foundered in sight of port, by a stroke
    of ironical Fate !

But the other owner was standing by, and, tossing her
    tangled locks,
Down she sat on the nearest seat—and took off her shoes
    and socks!
"One kiss, brother!" she murmured, "one clutch of your
    strong right hand—
And *I'll* paddle out to the *Puffin*, and bring her in safe to
    land!"

What can a barefooted child do? More than the pampered
    cur,
With his chicken-fed carcase shrinking, afraid from the
    bank to stir!
More than a baffled spaniel—aye, and more than the pug dog
    pet,
That wrinkles his ebony muzzle, and whines if his paws are
    wet!

"Come back!" the park-keeper shouted—but she merely
    answered, "I *won't!*"
And into the water she waded—though the invalids whim-
    pered, "Don't!"
Ah! but the Pond struck chilly, and the mud at the bottom
    was thick;
But in she paddled, and probed it with the point of a
    borrowed stick!

"Don't let go of me, darling!" "Keep hold of my fingers
    tight,
And I'll have it out in a minute or two . . . I haven't got
    up to it quite:
A minute more, and the sunken ship we'll safe to the sur-
    face bring,
Yes, and the sixpenny sailors, too, that we lashed to the
    funnel with string!"

Up to the knees in the water, Ethel and brother Ralph
Groped, till they *found* the *Puffin* and her sailors, soppy
    —but *safe!*
All the dear little sailors! . . . but—Children—I can't go on!
For poor old wooden-faced Noah was—*how* shall I tell you?
    —gone!

He must have fallen over, out of that heeling boat,
Away in the dim grey offing, to rise and to fall like a float,
Till the colour deserted his face and form, as it might at an
    infant's suck,
And he sank to his rest in his sailor's tomb—the maw of a
    hungry duck!

You are weeping? I cannot wonder. Mine *is* a pathetic
    style.
Weep for him, children, freely. . . . But, when you have
    finished, smile
With joy for his shipmates, rescued as though by a Pros-
    pero's wand,
And the *Puffin*, snatched from the slimy depths of the
    Round but treacherous Pond!

                         F. Anstey.

To Henrietta, on Her Departure for Calais   ~

WHEN little people go abroad, wherever they may roam,
    They will not just be treated as they used to be at
    home;
So take a few promiscuous hints, to warn you in advance,
Of how a little English girl will perhaps be served in France.

Of course you will be Frenchified ; and first, it's my belief,
They'll dress you in their foreign style as à-la-mode as beef,
With a little row of bee-hives, as a border to your frock,
And a pair of frilly trousers, like a little bantam cock.

But first they'll seize your bundle (if you have one) in a crack,
And tie it, with a tape, by way of bustle on your back ;
And make your waist so high or low, your shape will be a
 riddle,
For anyhow you'll never have your middle in the middle.

Your little English sandals for a while will hold together,
But woe betide you when the stones have worn away the
 leather ;
For they'll poke your little pettitoes (and there will be a
 hobble !)
In such a pair of shoes as none but carpenters can cobble !

You'll have to learn a *chou* is quite another sort of thing
To that you put your foot in ; that a *belle* is not to ring ;
That a *corne* is not the knubble that brings trouble to your
 toes,
Nor *peut-être* a potato, as some Irish folks suppose.

But pray, at meals, remember this, the French are so polite,
No matter what you eat and drink "whatever is, is right !"
So when you're told at dinner-time that some delicious stew
Is cat instead of rabbit, you must answer, " *Tant mi-eux* " !

Thomas Hood.

COUNSEL

Whole Duty of Children ❧

A CHILD should always say what's true
  And speak when he is spoken to,
And behave mannerly at table :
At least as far as he is able.

Robert Louis Stevenson.

Symon's Lesson of Wisdom
for all Manner of Children * ❧

CHILD, I warn thee in all wise,
  That thou tell truth and make no lies.
Child, be froward not, nor proud,
But raise thy head and speak aloud ;
When any man doth speak to thee,
Doff thy hood and bow thy knee ;
Wash thy hands and wash thy face,
And be thou courteous in each place.
When thou comest with good cheer
In hall or bower, bid " God be here ! "
Look thou cast at no man's dog
A stone, nor strike his horse or hog ;

---
* A fragment of a fifteenth-century poem, made modern.

Look thou neither scorn nor jape
With man, with maiden, nor with ape;
Let no man of thee make plaint;
Swear not by God, nor yet by saint.
Be courteous, when thou stand'st at meat,
And what men serve thee, take and eat:
Scrupling not to cry nor crave,
Saying, "Nay, *that* must I have."
Stand thou still before the board,
Look thou speak no noisy word.
Honour thy father and thy mother,
Grieve thou ne'er the one nor other;
But ever and oft shalt thou kneel down,
And ask their blessing and benisoun.
Child, keep thy clothes aye fair and clean,
Let no filth thereon be seen.
Child, climb not over house nor wall,
Neither for fruit, nor bird, nor ball.
Child, cast no stones at neighbour's house,
Since they may break his glass windows;
Make no noise, nor jape, nor play,
In holy church on holy day.
And, child, there's yet another thing,
Keep thee from words and jangeling.
And, child, whene'er thou goest to play,
Look thou come home by light of day.
I warn thee, child, of another matter,
Keep thee well from fire and water;
And beware of how thou dost look
Over brink, or well, or brook.

Rise betimes and go to school,
Fare not as a wanton fool,

Learn as fast as e'er thou can,
For our bishop good is an agèd man,
And therefore thou must learn right fast
Wouldst thou be bishop when he is past.

.   .   .   .   .

Symon.

The Introduction to " The Bad Child's Book of Beasts " ◟ ◟

I CALL you bad, my little child,
   Upon the title-page,
Because a manner rude and wild
   Is common at your age.

The Moral of this priceless work
   (If rightly understood)
Will make you—from a little Turk—
   Unnaturally good.

Do not as evil children do,
   Who on the slightest grounds
Will imitate the Kangaroo,
   With wild unmeaning bounds.

Do not, as children badly bred,
   Who eat like little Hogs,
And when they have to go to bed
   Will whine like Puppy Dogs:

Who take their manners from the Ape,
   Their habits from the Bear,
Indulge the loud unseemly jape,
   And never brush their hair.

But so control your actions that
    Your friends may all repeat,
" This child is dainty as the Cat,
    And as the Owl discreet."

Hilaire Belloc.

How to Look when Speaking ∽ ∽

" LOUISA, my love," Mrs. Manners began,
    " I fear you are learning to stare ;
To avoid looking bold, I must give you a plan,
    Quite easy to practise with care.

It is not a lady's or gentleman's eyes
    You should look at whenever address'd,
Whilst hearing them speak, or in making replies,
    To look at the *mouth* is the best.

This method is modest, and easy to learn
    When children are glad to be taught ;
And ah ! what a pleasure it is in return,
    To speak and to look as you ought ! "

Elizabeth Turner.

OLD-FASHIONED GIRLS

The Wonders ～ ～ ～ ～ ～

" MAMMA, dear mamma," cried, in haste, Mary Anne,
　　As into the parlour she eagerly ran,
" I hear that a giant is just come to town,
So tall, he is often oblig'd to stoop down;
O pray let us see him, O do let us go;
Indeed, dear mamma, he's a wonderful show."

"You are earnest, my love, and shall not be denied,"
Her truly affectionate mother replied.
" A lady this morning is also arrived,
Who of arms and of legs, from her birth was depriv'd,
And yet in a number of ways is expert,
As if she were blest with these limbs to exert.

"We'll visit Miss Beffin to-morrow, and then
I'll speak of the giant and lady again;
You are not mistaken, his overgrown size
We cannot behold, without feeling surprise,
Whilst Beffin's example most forcibly stands
A silent rebuke to all—*indolent hands.*"

Elizabeth Turner.

Maria's Purse 〜 〜 〜 〜

MARIA had an Aunt at Leeds,
  For whom she made a Purse of beads;
'Twas neatly done, by all allow'd,
And praise soon made her vain and proud.

Her mother, willing to repress
This strong conceit of cleverness,
Said, "I will show you, if you please,
A Honeycomb, the work of Bees!

"Yes, look within their hive, and then
Examine well your purse again;
Compare your merits, and you will
Admit the Insects' greater skill!"

Elizabeth Turner.

How to Write a Letter 〜 〜 〜

MARIA intended a letter to write,
  But could not begin (as she thought) to indite;
So went to her mother with pencil and slate,
Containing "Dear Sister," and also a date.

"With nothing to say, my dear girl, do not think
Of wasting your time over paper and ink;
But certainly this is an excellent way,
To try with your slate to find something to say.

'I will give you a rule," said her mother, "my dear,
Just think for a moment your sister is here,
And what would you tell her? consider, and then,
Though silent your tongue, you can speak with your pen."

Elizabeth Turner.

Rebecca's After-Thought

YESTERDAY, Rebecca Mason,
  In the parlour by herself,
Broke a handsome china basin,
  Plac'd upon the mantel-shelf.

Quite alarm'd, she thought of going
  Very quietly away,
Not a single person knowing,
  Of her being there that day.

But Rebecca recollected
  She was taught deceit to shun ;
And the moment she reflected,
  Told her mother what was done ;

Who commended her behaviour,
Lov'd her better, and forgave her.

Elizabeth Turner.

M

The Worm 〜 〜 〜

AS Sally sat upon the ground,
  A little crawling worm she found
    Among the garden dirt;
And when she saw the worm she scream'd,
And ran away and cried, and seem'd
    As if she had been hurt.

Mamma, afraid some serious harm
Made Sally scream, was in alarm,
    And left the parlour then;
But when the cause she came to learn,
She bade her daughter back return,
    To see the worm again.

The worm they found kept writhing round,
Until it sank beneath the ground;
    And Sally learned that day,
That worms are very harmless things,
With neither teeth, nor claws, nor stings
    To frighten her away.

Elizabeth Turner.

The Sash 〜 〜 〜

MAMMA had ordered Ann, the maid,
  Miss Caroline to wash;
And put on with her clean white frock,
  A handsome muslin sash.

But Caroline began to cry,
    For what you cannot think :
She said, " Oh, that's an ugly sash ;
    I'll have my pretty pink."

Papa, who in the parlour heard
    Her make the noise and rout,
That instant went to Caroline,
    To whip her, there's no doubt.

                    Elizabeth Turner.

The Lost Pudding

MISS Kitty was rude at the table one day,
    And would not sit still on her seat ;
Regardless of all that her mother could say,
From her chair little Kitty kept running away
    All the time they were eating their meat.

As soon as she saw that the beef was remov'd,
    She ran to her chair in great haste ;
But her mother such giddy behaviour reprov'd
By sending away the sweet pudding she lov'd,
    Without giving Kitty one taste.

                    Elizabeth Turner.

The Hoyden ～ ～ ～ ～ ～

MISS Agnes had two or three dolls, and a box
 To hold all her bonnets and tippets and frocks;
In a red leather thread-case that snapp'd when it shut,
She had needles to sew with and scissors to cut;
But Agnes lik'd better to play with rude boys,
Than work with her needle, or play with her toys.

Young ladies should always appear neat and clean,
Yet Agnes was seldom dress'd fit to be seen.
I saw her one morning attempting to throw
A very large stone, when it fell on her toe:
The boys who were present, and saw what was done,
Set up a loud laugh, and they call'd it fine fun.

But I took her home, and the doctor soon came,
And Agnes, I fear, will a long time be lame;
And from morning till night she laments very much,
That now when she walks she must lean on a crutch;
And she told her dear father, a thousand times o'er,
That she never will play with rude boys any more.

        Elizabeth Turner.

The Dizzy Girl ～ ～ ～ ～

AS Frances was playing and turning around,
 Her head grew so giddy she fell to the ground
'Twas well that she was not much hurt;

But, O what a pity! her frock was so soil'd
That had you beheld the unfortunate child,
   You had seen her all cover'd with dirt.

Her mother was sorry, and said, "Do not cry,
And Mary shall wash you, and make you quite dry,
   If you'll promise to turn round no more."
"What, not in the parlour?" the little girl said.
"No, not in the parlour; for lately I read
   Of a girl who was hurt with the door.

"She was playing and turning, until her poor head
Fell against the hard door, and it very much bled:
   And I heard Dr. Camomile tell,
That he put on a plaster, and cover'd it up;
Then he gave her some tea that was bitter to sup,
   Or perhaps it had never been well."

                    Elizabeth Turner.

The Giddy Girl

MISS Helen was always too giddy to heed
   What her mother had told her to shun;
For frequently, over the street in full speed,
   She would cross where the carriages run.

And out she would go to a very deep well,
   To look at the water below;
How naughty! to run to a dangerous well,
   Where her mother forbade her to go!

One morning, intending to take but one peep,
 Her foot slipp'd away from the ground ;
Unhappy misfortune ! the water was deep,
 And giddy Miss Helen was drown'd.
Elizabeth Turner.

Ambitious Sophy ᷄ ᷄ ᷄

MISS Sophy, one fine sunny day,
 Left her work and ran away ;
When soon she reach'd the garden-gate,
Which finding lock'd, she would not wait,
But tried to climb and scramble o'er
A gate as high as any door.

But little girls should never climb,
And Sophy won't another time ;
For when, upon the highest rail,
Her frock was caught upon a nail,
She lost her hold, and, sad to tell,
Was hurt and bruised—for down she fell.
Elizabeth Turner.

Poisonous Fruit ᷄ ᷄ ᷄

AS Tommy and his sister Jane
 Were walking down a shady lane,
They saw some berries, bright and red,
That hung around and over head ;

And soon the bough they bended down,
To make the scarlet fruit their own ;
And part they ate, and part, in play,
They threw about, and flung away.

But long they had not been at home
Before poor Jane and little Tom
Were taken sick, and ill, to bed,
And since, I've heard, they both are dead.

Alas ! had Tommy understood
That fruit in lanes is seldom good,
He might have walked with little Jane
Again along the shady lane.

Elizabeth Turner.

Playing with Fire   ∾   ∾

THE friends of little Mary Green
   Are now in deep distress,
The family will soon be seen
   To wear a mournful dress !

It seems from litter on the floor,
   She had been lighting straws,
Which caught the muslin frock she wore,
   A sad event to cause.

Her screams were loud and quickly heard,
   And remedies applied,
But all in vain, she scarcely stirr'd
   Again, before she died !

Elizabeth Turner.

False Alarms ～ ～ ～ ～

ONE day little Mary most loudly did call,
"Mamma! O mamma, pray come here;
A fall I have had, oh! a very sad fall."
Mamma ran in haste and in fear.

Then Mary jump'd up, and she laugh'd in great glee,
And cried, "Why, how fast you can run!
No harm has befall'n, I assure you, to me,
My screaming was only in fun."

Her mother was busy at work the next day;
She heard from without a loud cry:
"The great dog has got me! O help me! O pray!
He tears me, he bites me, I die!"

Mamma, all in terror, quick to the court flew,
And there little Mary she found;
Who, laughing, said, "Madam, pray how do you do?"
And curtsey'd quite down to the ground.

That night little Mary was some time in bed,
When cries and loud shrieking were heard:
"I'm on fire, O mamma! O come up, or I'm dead!"
Mamma, she believed not a word.

"Sleep, sleep, naughty child," she called out from below,
"How often have I been deceived!
You are telling a story, you very well know:
Go to sleep, for you can't be believed."

Yet still the child scream'd: now the house fill'd with smoke:
    That fire is above, Jane declares:
Alas! Mary's words they soon found were no joke,
    When ev'ry one hasten'd upstairs.

All burnt and all seam'd is her once pretty face,
    And terribly marked are her arms;
Her features all scarred, leave a lasting disgrace,
    For giving mamma false alarms.
                    Ann and Jane Taylor.

The Vulgar Little Lady

"BUT, mamma, now," said Charlotte, "pray, don't you
      believe
    That I'm better than Jenny, my nurse?
Only see my red shoes, and the lace on my sleeve;
    Her clothes are a thousand times worse.

"I ride in my coach, and have nothing to do,
    And the country folks stare at me so;
And nobody dares to control me but you,
    Because I'm a lady, you know.

"Then, servants are vulgar, and I am genteel;
    So, really, 'tis out of the way
To think that I should not be better a deal
    Than maids, and such people as they."

"Gentility, Charlotte," her mother replied,
   "Belongs to no station or place;
And nothing's so vulgar as folly and pride,
   Though dressed in red slippers and lace.

"Not all the fine things that fine ladies possess
   Should teach them the poor to despise;
For 'tis in good manners, and not in good dress,
   That the truest gentility lies."

Ann and Jane Taylor.

Meddlesome Matty

ONE ugly trick has often spoiled
   The sweetest and the best;
Matilda, though a pleasant child,
   One ugly trick possessed,
Which, like a cloud before the skies,
Hid all her better qualities.

Sometimes she'd lift the tea-pot lid,
   To peep at what was in it;
Or tilt the kettle, if you did
   But turn your back a minute.
In vain you told her not to touch,
Her trick of meddling grew so much.

Her grandmamma went out one day,
   And by mistake she laid
Her spectacles and snuff-box gay
   Too near the little maid;

"Ah! well," thought she, "I'll try them on,
As soon as grandmamma is gone."

Forthwith she placed upon her nose
 The glasses large and wide;
And looking round, as I suppose,
 The snuff-box too she spied:
"Oh! what a pretty box is that;
I'll open it," said little Matt.

"I know that grandmamma would say,
 'Don't meddle with it, dear';
But then, she's far enough away,
 And no one else is near:
Besides, what can there be amiss
In opening such a box as this?"

So thumb and finger went to work
 To move the stubborn lid,
And presently a mighty jerk
 The mighty mischief did;
For all at once, ah! woeful case,
The snuff came puffing in her face.

Poor eyes, and nose, and mouth beside
 A dismal sight presented;
In vain, as bitterly she cried,
 Her folly she repented.
In vain she ran about for ease;
She could do nothing now but sneeze.

She dashed the spectacles away,
 To wipe her tingling eyes,

And as in twenty bits they lay,
  Her grandmamma she spies.
" Heyday ! and what's the matter now ? "
Says grandmamma, with lifted brow.

Matilda, smarting with the pain,
  And tingling still, and sore,
Made many a promise to refrain
  From meddling evermore.
And 'tis a fact, as I have heard,
She ever since has kept her word.

Ann and Jane Taylor.

Frances keeps her Promise ∽

" MY Fanny, I have news to tell,
    Your diligence quite pleases me ;
You've worked so neatly, read so well,
    With Cousin Jane you may take tea.

" But pray remember this, my love,
    Although to stay you should incline,
And none but you should think to move,
    I wish you to return at nine."

With many thanks the attentive child
    Assured mamma she would obey :
Whom tenderly she kissed, and smiled,
    And with the maid then went away.

Arrived, the little girl was shown
    To where she met the merry band;
And when her coming was made known,
    All greet her with a welcome bland.

They dance, they play, and sweetly sing,
    In every sport each one partakes;
And now the servants sweetmeats bring,
    With wine and jellies, fruit and cakes.

Then comes papa, who says, "My dears,
    The magic-lantern if you'd see,
And that which on the wall appears,
    Leave off your play, and follow me."

While Frances too enjoyed the sight,
    Where moving figures all combine
To raise her wonder and delight,
    She hears, alas! the clock strike nine.

"Miss Fanny's maid for her is come."—
    "Oh dear, how soon!" the children cry,
They press, but Fanny will go home,
    And bids her little friends good-bye.

"See, dear mamma, I have not stayed";
    "Good girl, indeed," mamma replies,
"I knew you'd do as you had said,
    And now you'll find you've won a prize.

"So come, my love, and see the man
    Whom I desired at nine to call."
Downstairs young Frances quickly ran,
    And found him waiting in the hall.

"Here, Miss, are pretty birds to buy,
   A parrot or macaw so gay,
A speckled dove with scarlet eye :
   A linnet or a chattering jay.

"Would you a Java sparrow love?"
   "No, no, I thank you," said the child ;
"I'll have a beauteous cooing dove,
   So harmless, innocent, and mild."

"Your choice, my Fanny, I commend,
   Few birds can with the dove compare ;
But, lest it pine without a friend,
   I give you leave to choose a pair."

Ann and Jane Taylor.

MARJORIE FLEMING, POETESS

Ephibol on My Dear Love
Isabella 〜 〜 〜

HERE lies sweet Isabell in bed,
  With a night-cap on her head;
Her skin is soft, her face is fair,
And she has very pretty hair;
She and I in bed lie nice,
And undisturbed by rats and mice;
She is disgusted with Mr. Worgan,
Though he plays upon the organ.
Her nails are neat, her teeth are white,
Her eyes are very, very bright;
In a conspicuous town she lives,
And to the poor her money gives;
Here ends sweet Isabella's story,
And may it be much to her glory.

.　　.　　.　　.

I love in Isa's bed to lie,
Oh, such joy and luxury!
The bottom of the bed I sleep,
And with great care within I creep;
Oft I embrace her feet of lillys,
But she has gotten all the pillys.
Her neck I never can embrace,
But I do hug her feet in place.

Marjorie Fleming.

N

Sonnet to a Monkey ᔈ ᔈ

O LIVELY, O most charming pug,
  Thy graceful air, and heavenly mug;
The beauties of his mind do shine,
And every bit is shaped and fine.
Your teeth are whiter than the snow.
You're a great buck, you're a great beau;
Your eyes are of so nice a shape,
More like a Christian's than an ape;
Your cheek is like the rose's blume,
Your hair is like the raven's plume;
His nose's cast is of the Roman,
He is a very pretty woman.
I could not get a rhyme for Roman,
So was obliged to call him woman.

Marjorie Fleming.

OLD-FASHIONED BOYS

Going into Breeches ᦔ

JOY to Philip !—he this day
   Has his long coats cast away,
And (the childish season gone)
Puts the manly breeches on.
Officer on gay parade,
Red-coat in his first cockade,
Bridegroom in his wedding trim,
Birthday beau surpassing him,
Never did with conscious gait
Strut about in half the state,
Or the pride (yet free from sin)
Of my little mannikin :
Never was there pride, or bliss,
Half so rational as his.
Sashes, frocks, to those that need 'em—
Philip's limbs have got their freedom :
He can run, or he can ride,
And do twenty things beside,
Which his petticoats forbad :
Is he not a happy lad ?
Now he's under other banners,
He must leave his former manners :
Bid adieu to female games,

And forget their very names—
Puss-in-corners, hide-and-seek,
Sports for girls and punies weak!
Baste-the-bear he may now play at,
Leap-frog, football, sport away at;
Show his strength and skill at cricket—
Mark his distance, pitch his wicket;
Run about in winter's snow
Till his cheeks and fingers glow;
Climb a tree, or scale a wall,
Without any fear to fall;
If he get a hurt or bruise,
To complain he must refuse,
Though the anguish and the smart
Go unto his little heart;
He must have his courage ready,
Keep his voice and visage steady,
Brace his eyeballs stiff as drum,
That a tear may never come;
And his grief must only speak
From the colour in his cheek.
This, and more, he must endure—
Hero he in miniature!
This, and more, must now be done,
Now the breeches are put on.

Mary Lamb.

George and the Chimney-Sweep

HIS petticoats now George cast off,
  For he was four years old;
His trousers were of nankeen stuff,
  With buttons bright as gold.

"May I," said George, "just go abroad,
  My pretty clothes to show?
May I, mamma? but speak the word";
  The answer was, "No, no.

"Go, run below, George, in the court,
  But go not in the street,
Lest boys with you should make some sport,
  Or gipsies you should meet."
Yet, though forbidden, he went out,
  That other boys might spy,
And proudly there he walk'd about,
  And thought—"How fine am I!"

But whilst he strutted through the street,
  With looks both vain and pert,
A sweep-boy pass'd, whom not to meet,
  He slipped—into the dirt.
The sooty lad, whose heart was kind,
  To help him quickly ran,
And grasp'd his arm, with—"Never mind,
  You're up, my little man."

Sweep wiped his clothes with labour vain,
  And begged him not to cry;
And when he'd blacken'd every stain,
  Said, "Little sir, good-bye."
Poor George, almost as dark as sweep,
  And smear'd in dress and face,
Bemoans with sobs, both loud and deep,
  His well-deserved disgrace.

                    Ann and Jane Taylor.

Feigned Courage ∽ ∽

HORATIO, of ideal courage vain,
    Was flourishing in air his father's cane,
And, as the fumes of valour swelled his pate,
Now thought himself *this* hero, and now *that :*
"And now," he cried, "I will Achilles be ;
My sword I brandish ; see, the Trojans flee.
Now I'll be Hector, when his angry blade
A lane through heaps of slaughtered Grecians made !
And now by deeds still braver I'll evince,
I am no less than Edward the Black Prince.
Give way, ye coward French——!" As thus he spoke,
And aimed in fancy a sufficient stroke
To fix the fate of Cressy or Poictiers
(The nurse relates the hero's fate with tears) ;
He struck his milk-white hand against a nail,
Sees his own blood, and feels his courage fail.
Ah ! where is now that boasted valour flown,
That in the tented field so late was shown !
Achilles weeps, Great Hector hangs the head !
And the Black Prince goes whimpering to bed.
                                        Mary Lamb.

Politeness ∽ ∽ ∽

GOOD little boys should never say
    "I will," and "Give me these" ;
O, no ! that never is the way,
    But "Mother, if you please."

And "If you please," to Sister Ann
   Good boys to say are ready;
And, "Yes, sir," to a Gentleman,
   And, "Yes, ma'am," to a Lady.

Elizabeth Turner.

The Superior Boys ◡ ◡

TOM and Charles once took a walk,
   To see a pretty lamb;
And, as they went, began to talk
   Of little naughty Sam,

Who beat his younger brother, Bill,
   And threw him in the dirt;
And when his poor mamma was ill,
   He teascd her for a squirt.

"And I," said Tom, "won't play with Sam,
   Although he has a top":
But here the pretty little lamb
   To talking put a stop.

Elizabeth Turner.

The Lesson   →   →   →

ONE afternoon, as Joseph West,
    The boy who learnt his lesson best,
Was trying how his whip would crack,
By chance hit Headstrong on the back.

Enraged, he flew, and gave poor Joe
With all his might a sudden blow :
Nor would he listen to one word,
When Joe endeavoured to be heard.

Joe, finding him resolved to fight,
For what was accidental quite,
Although he never fought before,
Beat Headstrong till he'd have no more.

Elizabeth Turner.

Richard's Reformation   →

MISS Lucy was a charming child,
    She never said, " I won't ";
If little Dick her playthings spoil'd,
    She said, " Pray, Dicky, don't."

He took her waxen doll one day,
    And bang'd it round and round ;
Then tore its legs and arms away,
    And threw them on the ground.

His good mamma was angry quite,
  And Lucy's tears ran down;
But Dick went supperless that night,
  And since has better grown.

Elizabeth Turner.

The Cruel Boy ✺ ✺

RICHARD is a cruel boy,
  The people call him "Dick,"
For every day he seems to try
  Some new improper trick!

He takes delight in whipping cats,
  And pulling off their fur;
Although at first he gently pats,
  And listens to their purr.

A naughty boy! unless he mends
  He will be told to strip,
And learn how such amusement ends,
  By feeling his own whip.

Elizabeth Turner.

The Result of Cruelty ✺

JACK PARKER was a cruel boy,
  For mischief was his sole employ;
And much it grieved his friends to find
His thoughts so wickedly inclined.

He thought it clever to deceive,
And often ramble without leave;
And ev'ry animal he met
He dearly loved to plague and fret.

But all such boys, unless they mend,
May come to an unhappy end,
Like Jack, who got a fractured skull,
Whilst bellowing at a furious bull.

Elizabeth Turner.

Falsehood " Corrected "   ∾   ∾

WHEN Jacky drown'd our poor cat Tib,
    He told a very naughty fib,
And said he had not drown'd her;
But truth is always soon found out—
No one but Jack had been about
    The place where Thomas found her.

And Thomas saw him with the cat
(Though Jacky did not know of that),
    And told papa the trick;
He saw him take a slender string,
And round poor Pussy's neck then swing
    A very heavy brick.

His parents, being very sad
To find they had a boy so bad,
    To say what was not true,

Determined to correct him then;
And never was he known again
   Such naughty things to do.

                Elizabeth Turner.

The Greedy Boy ᵔ ᵔ ᵔ

SAMMY SMITH would drink and eat
   From morning until night;
He filled his mouth so full of meat,
   It was a shameful sight.

Sometimes he gave a book or toy
   For apple, cake, or plum;
And grudged if any other boy
   Should taste a single crumb.

Indeed he ate and drank so fast,
   And used to stuff and cram,
The name they call'd him by at last
   Was often Greedy Sam.

                Elizabeth Turner.

Greedy Richard ᵔ ᵔ ᵔ

" I THINK I want some pies this morning,"
   Said Dick, stretching himself and yawning;
So down he threw his slate and books,
And sauntered to the pastry-cook's.

And there he cast his greedy eyes
Round on the jellies and the pies,
So to select, with anxious care,
The very nicest that was there.

At last the point was thus decided :
As his opinion was divided
'Twixt pie and jelly, being loth
Either to leave, he took them both.

Now, Richard never could be pleased
To stop when hunger was appeased,
But would go on to eat still more
When he had had an ample store.

" No, not another now," said Dick ;
" Dear me, I feel extremely sick :
I cannot even eat this bit ;
I wish I had not tasted it."

Then slowly rising from his seat,
He threw his cheesecake in the street,
And left the tempting pastry-cook's
With very discontented looks.

Just then a man with wooden leg
Met Dick, and held his hat to beg ;
And while he told his mournful case
Looked at him with imploring face.

Dick, wishing to relieve his pain,
His pockets searched, but searched in vain ;
And so at last he did declare,
He had not left a farthing there.

The beggar turned with face of grief,
And look of patient unbelief,
While Richard now his folly blamed,
And felt both sorry and ashamed.

" I wish," said he (but wishing's vain),
" I had my money back again,
And had not spent my last, to pay
For what I only threw away.

" Another time I'll take advice,
And not buy things because they're nice ;
But rather save my little store,
To give to those who want it more."

Ann and Jane Taylor.

The Plum-Cake ∽ ∽ ∽ ∽ ∽

" OH ! I've got a plum-cake, and a fine feast I'll make,
    So nice to have all to myself !
I can eat every day while the rest are at play,
    And then put it by on the shelf."

Thus said little John, and how soon it was gone !
    For with zeal to his cake he applied,
While fingers and thumbs, for the sweetmeats and plums,
    Were hunting and digging beside.

But, woeful to tell, a misfortune befell,
    That shortly his folly reveal'd :
After eating his fill, he was taken so ill,
    That the cause could not now be conceal'd.

As he grew worse and worse, the doctor and nurse
　　To cure his disorder were sent;
And rightly you'll think, he had physic to drink,
　　Which made him sincerely repent.

And while on the bed he roll'd his hot head,
　　Impatient with sickness and pain,
He could not but take this reproof from his cake,
　　"Do not be such a glutton again."

Ann and Jane Taylor.

Another Plum-Cake ～ ～ ～ ～

"OH! I've got a plum-cake, and a feast let us make;
　　Come, schoolfellows, come at my call;
I assure you 'tis nice, and we'll each have a slice,
　　Here's more than enough for us all."

Thus said little Jack, as he gave it a smack,
　　And sharpen'd his knife to begin;
Nor was there one found, upon the play-ground,
　　So cross that he would not come in.

With masterly strength he cut through it at length,
　　And gave to each playmate a share:
Charles, William, and James, and many more names,
　　Partook his benevolent care.

And when it was done, and they'd finished their fun,
　　To marbles or hoop they went back;
And each little boy felt it always a joy,
　　To do a good turn for good Jack.

In his task and his book, his best pleasures he took,
    And as he thus wisely began,
Since he's been a man grown he has constantly shown
    That a good boy will make a good man.

                        Ann and Jane Taylor.

The Little Fisherman

THERE was a little fellow once,
    And Harry was his name ;
And many a naughty trick had he,
    I tell it to his shame.

He minded not his friends' advice,
    But followed his own wishes ;
And one most cruel trick of his
    Was that of catching fishes.

His father had a little pond,
    Where often Harry went ;
And there, in this unfeeling sport,
    He many an evening spent.

One day he took his hook and bait,
    And hurried to the pond,
And there began the cruel game,
    Of which he was so fond.

And many a little fish he caught,
    And pleased was he to look
To see them writhe in agony
    And struggle on the hook.

o

At last, when having caught enough,
    And also tired himself,
He hasten'd home, intending there
    To put them on a shelf.

But as he jump'd to reach a dish,
    To put his fishes in,
A large meat-hook, that hung close by,
    Did catch him by the chin.

Poor Harry kick'd, and call'd aloud,
    And scream'd, and cried, and roar'd,
While from his wound the crimson blood
    In dreadful torrents pour'd.

The maids came running, frighten'd much
    To see him hanging there,
And soon they took him from the hook,
    And set him in a chair.

The surgeon came and stopp'd the blood,
    And bound his aching head ;
And then they carried him upstairs,
    And laid him on his bed.

Conviction darted on his mind,
    As groaning there he lay,
And with compunction then he thought
    About his cruel play.

"And oh," said he, "poor little fish,
    What tortures they have borne :
While I, well pleased, have stood to see
    Their tender bodies torn !

"Though fishermen must earn their bread,
  And butchers too must slay,
That can be no excuse for me,
  Who do the same in play.

" But now I know how great the smart,
  How terrible the pain !
I think, while I can feel myself,
  I will not fish again."

                              Ann and Jane Taylor.

The Two Gardens

WHEN Harry and Dick had been striving to please,
    Their father (to whom it was known)
Made two little gardens, and stocked them with trees,
    And gave one to each for his own.

Harry thank'd his papa, and with rake, hoe, and spade,
    Directly began his employ :
And soon such a neat little garden was made,
    That he panted with labour and joy.

There was always some bed or some border to mend,
    Or something to tie or to stick ;
And Harry rose early his garden to tend,
    While sleeping lay indolent Dick.

The tulip, the rose, and the lily so white,
    United their beautiful bloom :
And often the honey-bee stooped from his flight
    To sip the delicious perfume.

A neat row of peas in full blossom was seen,
  French beans were beginning to shoot ;
And his gooseberries and currants, though yet they were
    green,
  Foretold for him plenty of fruit.

But Richard loved better in bed to repose,
  And there, as he curl'd himself round,
Forgot that no tulip, nor lily, nor rose,
  Nor fruit in his garden was found.

Rank weeds and tall nettles disfigured his beds,
  Nor cabbage nor lettuce was seen :
The slug and the snail showed their mischievous heads,
  And ate every leaf that was green.

Thus Richard the idle, who shrank from the cold,
  Beheld his trees naked and bare ;
While Harry the active was charmed to behold
  The fruit of his patience and care.

Ann and Jane Taylor.

The Truant Boys   ∽   ∽   ∽   ∽

THE month was August and the morning cool,
    When Hal and Ned,
To walk together to the neighbouring school,
  Rose early from their bed.

When near the school Hal said, "Why con your task,
  Demure and prim ?
Ere we go in, let me one question ask,
  Ned, shall we go and swim ?"

Fearless of future punishment and blame,
   Away they hied,
Through many a verdant field, until they came
   Unto the river's side.

The broad stream narrow'd in its onward course,
   And deep and still
It silent ran, and yet with rapid force,
   To turn a neighbouring mill.

Under the mill an arch gaped wide, and seem'd
   The jaws of death!
Through this the smooth deceitful waters teemed
   On dreadful wheels beneath.

They swim the river wide, nor think nor care:
   The waters flow,
And by the current strong they carried are
   Into the mill-stream now.

Through the swift waters as young Ned was roll'd,
   The gulf when near,
On a kind brier by chance he laid fast hold,
   And stopped his dread career.

But luckless Hal was by the mill-wheel torn;—
   A warning sad!
And the untimely death all friends now mourn,
   Of this poor truant lad.

                  Ann and Jane Taylor.

The Boys and the Apple Tree ∽ ∽

AS William and Thomas were walking one day,
  They came by a fine orchard's side :
They would rather eat apples than spell, read, or play,
  And Thomas to William then cried :

"O brother, look yonder ! what clusters hang there !
  I'll try and climb over the wall :
I must have an apple ; I will have a pear ;
  Although it should cost me a fall ! "

Said William to Thomas, " To steal is a sin,
  Mamma has oft told this to thee :
I never have stole, nor will I begin,
  So the apples may hang on the tree."

"You are a good boy, as you ever have been,"
  Said Thomas, "let's walk on, my lad :
We'll call on our schoolfellow, Benjamin Green,
  Who to see us I know will be glad."

They came to the house, and asked at the gate,
  "Is Benjamin Green now at home ? "
But Benjamin did not allow them to wait,
  And brought them both into the room.

And he smiled, and he laugh'd, and he caper'd with joy,
  His little companions to greet :
"And we too are happy," said each little boy,
  "Our playfellow dear thus to meet."

" Come, walk in our garden, this morning so fine,
 We may, for my father gives leave ;
And more, he invites you to stay here and dine :
 And a most happy day we shall have ! "

But when in the garden, they found 'twas the same
 They saw as they walk'd in the road ;
And near the high wall when those little boys came,
 They started as if from a toad.

" That large ring of iron you see on the ground,
 With terrible teeth like a saw,"
Said their friend, " the guard of our garden is found,
 And it keeps all intruders in awe.

" If any the warning without set at nought,
 Their legs then this man-trap must tear " :
Said William to Thomas, " So you'd have been caught,
 If you had leap'd over just there."

Cried Thomas, in terror of what now he saw,
 " With my faults I will heartily grapple ;
For I learn what may happen by breaking a law,
 Although but in stealing an apple."

      Ann and Jane Taylor.

James and the Shoulder of Mutton   ∽

YOUNG Jem at noon returned from school,
 As hungry as could be,
He cried to Sue, the servant-maid,
 " My dinner give to me."

Said Sue, "It is not yet come home;
  Besides, it is not late."
"No matter that," cries little Jem,
  "I do not like to wait."

Quick to the baker's Jemmy went,
  And ask'd, "Is dinner done?"
"It is," replied the baker's man.
  "Then home I'll with it run."

"Nay, sir," replied he prudently,
  "I tell you 'tis too hot,
And much too heavy 'tis for you."
  "I tell you it is not.

"Papa, mamma, are both gone out,
  And I for dinner long;
So give it me, it is all mine,
  And, baker, hold your tongue.

"A shoulder 'tis of mutton nice!
  And batter-pudding too;
I'm glad of that, it is so good;
  How clever is our Sue!"

Now near the door young Jem was come,
  He round the corner turn'd,
But oh, sad fate! unlucky chance!
  The dish his fingers burn'd.

Low in the kennel down fell dish,
  And down fell all the meat:
Swift went the pudding in the stream,
  And sail'd along the street.

The people laugh'd, and rude boys grinned
  At mutton's hapless fall ;
But though ashamed, young Jemmy cried,
  " Better lose part than all."

The shoulder by the knuckle seized,
  His hands both grasp'd it fast,
And deaf to all their gibes and cries,
  He gain'd his home at last.

" Impatience is a fault," cries Jem,
  " The baker told me true :
In future I will patient be,
  And mind what says our Sue."

Ann and Jane Taylor.

Rudeness ❧ ❧ ❧ ❧ ❧ ❧

JAMES went to the door of the kitchen and said,
  " Cook, give me this moment some honey and bread ;
Then fetch me a glass or a cup of good beer,
Why, cook, you don't stir, and I'm sure you must hear ! "

" Indeed, Master James," was the cook's right reply,
" To answer such language I feel rather shy,
I hear you quite plainly, but wait till you choose
To civilly ask, when I shall not refuse."

What pity young boys should indulge in this way,
Whilst knowing so well what is proper to say ;
As if civil words, in a well-manner'd tone,
Were learn'd to be us'd in the parlour alone !

Elizabeth Turner.

The Models ❧ ❧ ❧

AS Dick and Bryan were at play
   At trap, it came to pass,
Dick struck the ball, so far away,
   He broke a pane of glass.

Though much alarmed, they did not run,
   But walk'd up to the spot;
And offer'd for the damage done
   What money they had got.

When accidents like this arise,
   Dear children! this rely on,
All honest, honourable boys
   Will act like Dick and Bryan.

Elizabeth Turner

LOOKING FORWARD

The Lamplighter ✑ ✑ ✑ ✑

M Y tea is nearly ready and the sun has left the sky;
　　It's time to take the window to see Leerie going by;
For every night at tea time and before you take your seat,
With lantern and with ladder he comes posting up the street.

Now Tom would be a driver and Maria go to sea,
And my papa's a banker and as rich as he can be;
But I, when I am stronger and can choose what I'm to do,
O Leerie, I'll go round at night and light the lamps with
　　　you!

For we are very lucky, with a lamp before the door,
And Leerie stops to light it as he lights so many more;
And O! before you hurry by with ladder and with light,
O Leerie, see a little child and nod to him to-night!

Robert Louis Stevenson.

The Pedlar's Caravan ✑ ✑ ✑

I WISH I lived in a caravan,
　　With a horse to drive, like a pedlar-man!
Where he comes from nobody knows,
Or where he goes to, but on he goes!

His caravan has windows two,
And a chimney of tin, that the smoke comes through ;
He has a wife, with a baby brown,
And they go riding from town to town.

Chairs to mend, and delf to sell !
He clashes the basins like a bell ;
Tea-trays, baskets ranged in order,
Plates with the alphabet round the border !

The roads are brown, and the sea is green,
But his house is just like a bathing-machine ;
The world is round, and he can ride,
Rumble and splash, to the other side !

With the pedlar-man I should like to roam,
And write a book when I came home ;
All the people would read my book,
Just like the Travels of Captain Cook !

W. B. Rands.

A Shooting Song ◦ ◦ ◦

TO shoot, to shoot, would be my delight,
  To shoot the cats that howl in the night ;
To shoot the lion, the wolf, the bear,
To shoot the mad dogs out in the square.

I learnt to shoot with a pop-gun good,
Made out of a branch of elder wood ;
It was round, and long, full half a yard,
The plug was strong, the pellets were hard.

I should like to shoot with a bow of yew,
As the English at Agincourt used to do ;
The strings of a thousand bows went twang,
And a thousand arrows whizzed and sang !

On Hounslow Heath I should like to ride,
With a great horse-pistol at my side :
It is dark—hark ! A robber, I know !
Click ! crick-crack ! and away we go !

I will shoot with a double-barrelled gun,
Two bullets are better than only one ;
I will shoot some rooks to put in a pie ;
I will shoot an eagle up in the sky.

I once shot a bandit—in a dream—
In a mountain pass I heard a scream ;
I rescued the lady, and set her free,
" Do not fear, madam, lean on me ! "

With a boomerang I could not aim ;
A poison blow-pipe would be the same ;
A double-barrelled is my desire,
Get out of the way—one, two, three, fire !

W. B. Rands.

The Boy Decides ᕒ ᕒ

I 'D like to be a p'liceman
    And flash my bull's-eye out,—
If there were not so many thieves
    And drunken men about.

I'd like to be a butcher
   And use a knife and steel,—
If only bullocks didn't bleed
   And piggies wouldn't squeal.

And sailors go so far from home.
   And soldiers often die,
And Mr. Blake, the blacksmith,
   Got a big spark in his eye ;

And so I think that, after all,
   I'll be a railway guard,
And run beside the train, and jump,
   And blow my whistle hard.

Rickman Mark

FROM "HIAWATHA"

Hiawatha's Childhood

BY the shores of Gitche Gumee,
By the shining Big-Sea-Water,
Stood the wigwam of Nokomis,
Daughter of the Moon, Nokomis.
Dark behind it rose the forest,
Rose the black and gloomy pine-trees,
Rose the firs with cones upon them;
Bright before it beat the water,
Beat the clear and sunny water,
Beat the shining Big-Sea-Water.
   There the wrinkled old Nokomis
Nursed the little Hiawatha,
Rocked him in his linden cradle,
Bedded soft in moss and rushes,
Safely bound with reindeer sinews;
Stilled his fretful wail by saying,
"Hush! the Naked Bear will hear thee!"
Lulled him into slumber, singing,
"Ewa-yea! my little owlet!
Who is this, that lights the wigwam?
With his great eyes lights the wigwam?
Ewa-yea! my little owlet!"
   Many things Nokomis taught him
Of the stars that shine in heaven;

Showed him Ishkoodah, the comet,
Ishkoodah, with fiery tresses;
Showed the Death-Dance of the spirits,
Warriors with their plumes and war-clubs,
Flaring far away to northward
In the frosty nights of Winter;
Showed the broad white road in heaven,
Pathway of the ghosts, the shadows,
Running straight across the heavens,
Crowded with the ghosts, the shadows.

At the door on summer evenings
Sat the little Hiawatha;
Heard the whispering of the pine-trees,
Heard the lapping of the waters,
Sounds of music, words of wonder;
"Minne-wawa!" said the pine-trees,
"Mudway-aushka!" said the water.

Saw the fire-fly, Wah-wah-taysee,
Flitting through the dusk of evening,
With the twinkle of its candle
Lighting up the brakes and bushes,
And he sang the song of children,
Sang the song Nokomis taught him:
"Wah-wah-taysee, little fire-fly,
Little, flitting, white-fire insect,
Little, dancing, white-fire creature,
Light me with your little candle,
Ere upon my bed I lay me,
Ere in sleep I close my eyelids!"

Saw the moon rise from the water
Rippling, rounding from the water,
Saw the flecks and shadows on it,
Whispered, "What is that, Nokomis?"

And the good Nokomis answered:
"Once a warrior, very angry,
Seized his grandmother, and threw her
Up into the sky at midnight;
Right against the moon he threw her;
'Tis her body that you see there."
    Saw the rainbow in the heaven,
In the eastern sky, the rainbow,
Whispered, "What is that, Nokomis?"
And the good Nokomis answered:
"'Tis the heaven of flowers you see there;
All the wild-flowers of the forest,
All the lilies of the prairie,
When on earth they fade and perish,
Blossom in that heaven above us."
    When he heard the owls at midnight,
Hooting, laughing in the forest,
"What is that?" he cried in terror,
"What is that?" he said, "Nokomis?"
And the good Nokomis answered:
"That is but the owl and owlet,
Talking in their native language,
Talking, scolding at each other."
    Then the little Hiawatha
Learned of every bird its language,
Learned their names and all their secrets,
How they built their nests in Summer,
Where they hid themselves in Winter,
Talked with them whene'er he met them,
Called them "Hiawatha's Chickens."
    Of all beasts he learned the language,
Learned their names and all their secrets,
How the beavers built their lodges,

Where the squirrels hid their acorns,
How the reindeer ran so swiftly,
Why the rabbit was so timid,
Talked with them whene'er he met them,
Called them "Hiawatha's Brothers."
    Then Iagoo, the great boaster,
He the marvellous story-teller,
He the traveller and the talker,
He the friend of old Nokomis,
Made a bow for Hiawatha;
From a branch of ash he made it,
From an oak-bough made the arrows,
Tipped with flint, and winged with feathers,
And the cord he made of deerskin.
    Then he said to Hiawatha:
"Go, my son, into the forest,
Where the red deer herd together,
Kill for us a famous roebuck,
Kill for us a deer with antlers!"
    Forth into the forest straightway
All alone walked Hiawatha
Proudly, with his bow and arrows;
And the birds sang round him, o'er him,
"Do not shoot us, Hiawatha!"
Sang the robin, the Opechee,
Sang the bluebird, the Owaissa,
"Do not shoot us, Hiawatha!"
    Up the oak-tree, close beside him,
Sprang the squirrel, Adjidaumo,
In and out among the branches,
Coughed and chattered from the oak-tree,
Laughed, and said between his laughing,
"Do not shoot me, Hiawatha!"

And the rabbit from his pathway
Leaped aside, and at a distance
Sat erect upon his haunches,
Half in fear, and half in frolic,
Saying to the little hunter,
" Do not shoot me, Hiawatha ! "
    But he heeded not, nor heard them,
For his thoughts were with the red deer ;
On their tracks his eyes were fastened,
Leading downward to the river,
To the ford across the river,
And as one in slumber walked he.
    Hidden in the alder-bushes,
There he waited till the deer came,
Till he saw two antlers lifted,
Saw two eyes look from the thicket,
Saw two nostrils point to windward,
And a deer came down the pathway,
Flecked with leafy light and shadow.
And his heart within him fluttered,
Trembled like the leaves above him,
Like the birch-leaf palpitated,
As the deer came down the pathway.
    Then, upon one knee uprising,
Hiawatha aimed an arrow ;
Scarce a twig moved with his motion,
Scarce a leaf was stirred or rustled,
But the wary roebuck started,
Stamped with all his hoofs together,
Listened with one foot uplifted,
Leaped as if to meet the arrow ;
Ah ! the singing, fatal arrow,
Like a wasp it buzzed and stung him !

Dead he lay there in the forest,
By the ford across the river;
Beat his timid heart no longer,
But the heart of Hiawatha
Throbbed and shouted and exulted,
As he bore the red deer homeward,
And Iagoo and Nokomis
Hailed his coming with applauses.

From the red deer's hide Nokomis
Made a cloak for Hiawatha,
From the red deer's flesh Nokomis
Made a banquet in his honour.
All the village came and feasted,
All the guests praised Hiawatha,
Called him Strong-Heart, Soan-ge-taha!
Called him Loon-Heart, Mahn-go-taysee!

H. W. Longfellow.

Hiawatha's Sailing

"GIVE me of your bark, O Birch-tree!
  Of your yellow bark, O Birch-tree!
Growing by the rushing river,
Tall and stately in the valley!
I a light canoe will build me,
Build a swift Cheemaun for sailing,
That shall float upon the river,
Like a yellow leaf in Autumn,
Like a yellow water-lily!

"Lay aside your cloak, O Birch-tree!
Lay aside your white-skin wrapper,

For the Summer-time is coming,
And the sun is warm in heaven,
And you need no white-skin wrapper!"
  Thus aloud cried Hiawatha
In the solitary forest,
By the rushing Taquamenaw,
When the birds were singing gaily,
In the Moon of Leaves were singing,
And the sun, from sleep awaking,
Started up and said, "Behold me!
Geezis, the great Sun, behold me!"
  And the tree with all its branches
Rustled in the breeze of morning,
Saying, with a sigh of patience,
"Take my cloak, O Hiawatha!"
  With his knife the tree he girdled;
Just beneath its lowest branches,
Just above the roots, he cut it,
Till the sap came oozing outward;
Down the trunk, from top to bottom,
Sheer he cleft the bark asunder,
With a wooden wedge he raised it,
Stripped it from the trunk unbroken.
  "Give me of your boughs, O Cedar!
Of your strong and pliant branches,
My canoe to make more steady,
Make more strong and firm beneath me!"
  Through the summit of the Cedar
Went a sound, a cry of horror,
Went a murmur of resistance;
But it whispered, bending downward,
"Take my boughs, O Hiawatha!"
  Down he hewed the boughs of cedar,

Shaped them straightway to a frame-work,
Like two bows he formed and shaped them,
Like two bended bows together.
    "Give me of your roots, O Tamarack!
Of your fibrous roots, O Larch-tree!
My canoe to bind together,
So to bind the ends together
That the water may not enter,
That the river may not wet me!"
    And the Larch, with all its fibres,
Shivered in the air of morning,
Touched his forehead with its tassels,
Said, with one long sigh of sorrow,
"Take them all, O Hiawatha!"
    From the earth he tore the fibres,
Tore the tough roots of the Larch-tree,
Closely sewed the bark together,
Bound it closely to the frame-work.
    "Give me of your balm, O Fir-tree
Of your balsam and your resin,
So to close the seams together
That the water may not enter,
That the river may not wet me!"
    And the Fir-tree, tall and sombre,
Sobbed through all its robes of darkness,
Rattled like a shore with pebbles,
Answered wailing, answered weeping,
"Take my balm, O Hiawatha!"
    And he took the tears of balsam,
Took the resin of the Fir-tree,
Smeared therewith each seam and fissure,
Made each crevice safe from water.
    "Give me of your quills, O Hedgehog!

All your quills, O Kagh, the Hedgehog!
I will make a necklace of them,
Make a girdle for my beauty,
And two stars to deck her bosom!"
From a hollow tree the Hedgehog
With his sleepy eyes looked at him,
Shot his shining quills, like arrows,
Saying, with a drowsy murmur,
Through the tangle of his whiskers,
"Take my quills, O Hiawatha!"
From the ground the quills he gathered,
All the little shining arrows,
Stained them red and blue and yellow,
With the juice of roots and berries;
Into his canoe he wrought them,
Round its waist a shining girdle,
Round its bows a gleaming necklace,
On its breast two stars resplendent.
Thus the Birch-Canoe was builded
In the valley, by the river,
In the bosom of the forest;
And the forest's life was in it,
All its mystery and its magic,
All the lightness of the Birch-tree,
All the toughness of the Cedar,
All the Larch's supple sinews;
And it floated on the river
Like a yellow leaf in Autumn,
Like a yellow water-lily.
Paddles none had Hiawatha,
Paddles none he had or needed,
For his thoughts as paddles served him,
And his wishes served to guide him;

Swift or slow at will he glided,
Veered to right or left at pleasure.
　Then he called aloud to Kwasind,
To his friend, the strong man, Kwasind,
Saying, " Help me clear this river
Of its sunken logs and sand-bars."
　Straight into the river Kwasind
Plunged as if he were an otter,
Dived as if he were a beaver,
Stood up to his waist in water,
To his arm-pits in the river,
Swam and shouted in the river,
Tugged at sunken logs and branches,
With his hands he scooped the sand-bars,
With his feet the ooze and tangle.
　And thus sailed my Hiawatha
Down the rushing Taquamenaw,
Sailed through all its bends and windings,
Sailed through all its deeps and shallows,
While his friend, the strong man, Kwasind,
Swam the deeps, the shallows waded.
　Up and down the river went they,
In and out among its islands,
Cleared its bed of root and sand-bar,
Dragged the dead trees from its channel,
Made its passage safe and certain,
Made a pathway for the people,
From its springs among the mountains,
To the waters of Pauwating,
To the bay of Taquamenaw.

H. W. Longfellow.

GOOD FELLOWS

The Jovial Cobbler of Saint Helen's ∽ ∽

I AM a jovial cobbler, bold and brave,
  And as for employment, enough I have
For to keep jogging my hammer and my awl,
Whilst I sit singing and whistling in my stall.

But there's Dick the carman, and Hodge, who drives the
      dray
For sixteen or eighteen pence a day,
They slave in the dirt, whilst I, with my awl,
Do get more money sitting, singing, whistling in my stall.

And there's Tom the porter, companion of the pot,
Who stands in the street, with his rope and knot,
Waiting in a corner to hear who will him call,
Whilst I am getting money, money, money in my stall.

And there's the jolly broom-man, his bread for to get,
Cries "Brooms" up and down in the open street,
And one cries "Broken glasses, though never so small,"
Whilst I am getting money, money, money in my stall.

And there is a gang of poor smutty souls,
Who trudge up and down, to cry "Small coals,"
With a sack on their back, at the door stand and call,
Whilst I am getting money, money, money in my stall.

And others there are with another note,
Who cry up and down, " An old suit or coat,"
And perhaps, on some days, they get nothing at all,
Whilst I sit singing, getting money, money in my stall.

And there's a jolly cooper, with hoops at his back,
Who trudgeth up and down to see who lack
Their casks to be made tight, with hoops great and small,
Whilst I sit singing, getting money, money in my stall.

And there's a jolly tinker, who loves a bonny lass,
Who trudges up and down to mend old brass,
With his long smutty pouch, to force holes withal,
Whilst I sit singing, getting money, money in my stall.

And there's another, call'd old Tommy Terrah,
Who, up and down the city, does drive with a barrow,
To try to sell his fruit to great and to small,
Whilst I sit singing, getting money, money in my stall.

And there are the blind, and the lame with wooden leg,
Who up and down the city are forced to beg :
They get crumbs of comfort, the which are but small,
Whilst I sit singing, getting money, money in my stall.

And there's a gang of wenches, who oysters do sell ;
And then Powder Moll, with her scent-sweet smell ;
She trudges up and down with powder and with ball,
Whilst I sit singing, getting money, money in my stall. ·

And there are jovial girls with their milking-pails,
Who trudge up and down, with their draggle-tails
Flip-flapping at their heels ; for customers they call,
Whilst I sit singing, getting money, money in my stall.

These are the gang who do take great pain,
And it is these who me maintain,
But when it blows and rains, I do pity them all
To see them trudge about, while I am in my stall.

And there are many more who slave and toil,
Their living to get, but it's not worth while
To mention them all; so I'll sing in my stall,
I am the happiest mortal, mortal of them all.

Old Song.

The Jovial Beggar 〜 〜

THERE was a jovial beggar,
   He had a wooden leg,
Lame from his cradle,
   And forced for to beg.
And a-begging we will go, will go, will go,
And a-begging we will go!

A bag for his oatmeal,
   Another for his salt,
And a pair of crutches,
   To show that he can halt.
And a-begging we will go—

A bag for his wheat,
   Another for his rye,
A little bottle by his side
   To drink when he's a-dry.
And a-begging we will go—

Q

Seven years I begged
  For my old Master Wild,
He taught me to beg
  When I was but a child.
And a-begging we will go—

I begged for my master,
  And got him store of pelf;
But now, Jove be praised!
  I'm begging for myself.
And a-begging we will go—

In a hollow tree
  I live and pay no rent—
Providence provides for me,
  And I am well content.
And a-begging we will go—

Of all the occupations,
  A beggar's life's the best,
For whenever he's a-weary,
  He'll lay him down and rest.
And a-begging we will go—

I fear no plots against me,
  I live in open cell;
Then who would be a king,
  When beggars live so well?
And a-begging we will go, will go, will go,
And a-begging we will go!

Old Song.

The Lincolnshire Poacher ～ ～ ～ ～

WHEN I was bound apprentice, in famous Lincolnshire,
Full well I serv'd my master for more than seven year,
Till I took up to poaching, as you shall quickly hear.
Oh! 'tis my delight on a shining night, in the season of the
year.

As me and my comarade were setting of a snare,
'Twas then we spied the gamekeeper, for him we did not care,
For we can wrestle and fight, my boys, and jump o'er any-
where.
Oh! 'tis my delight on a shining night, in the season of the
year.

As me and my comarade were setting four or five,
And taking on 'em up again, we caught a hare alive,
We took the hare alive, my boys, and thro' the woods did
steer.
Oh! 'tis my delight on a shining night, in the season of the
year.

I threw him on my shoulder, and then we trudged home,
We took him to a neighbour's house, and sold him for a
crown,
We sold him for a crown, my boys, but I did not tell you
where.
Oh! 'tis my delight on a shining night, in the season of the
year.

Success to every gentleman that lives in Lincolnshire,
Success to every poacher that wants to sell a hare,
Bad luck to every gamekeeper that will not sell his deer.
Oh! 'tis my delight on a shining night in the season of the
year.

Old Song.

The Old Courtier ◡ ◡ ◡ ◡ ◡

A N old song made by an aged old pate,
　　Of an old worshipful gentleman who had a great estate,
That kept a brave old house at a bountiful rate,
And an old porter to relieve the poor at his gate ;
　　　　Like an old courtier of the Queen's,
　　　　And the Queen's old courtier.

With an old lady, whose anger one word assuages,
They every quarter paid their old servants their wages,
And never knew what belong'd to coachmen, footmen, nor
　　pages,
But kept twenty old fellows with blue coats and badges ;
　　　　Like an old courtier—

With an old study fill'd full of learned old books,
With an old reverend chaplain, you might know him by his
　　looks,
With an old buttery hatch worn quite off the hooks,
And an old kitchen, that maintain'd half a dozen old cooks;
　　　　Like an old courtier—

With an old hall, hung about with pikes, guns, and bows,
With old swords, and bucklers, that had borne many shrewd
　　blows,
And an old frieze coat, to cover his worship's trunk hose,
And a cup of old sherry to comfort his copper nose ;
　　　　Like an old courtier—

With a good old fashion, when Christmas was come,
To call in all his old neighbours with bagpipe and drum,

With good cheer enough to furnish every old room,
And old liquor able to make a cat speak, and man dumb;
      Like an old courtier—

With an old falconer, huntsman, and a kennel of hounds,
That never hawk'd, nor hunted, but in his own grounds,
Who, like a wise man, kept himself within his own bounds,
And when he died gave every child a thousand good pounds;
      Like an old courtier of the Queen's,
      And the Queen's old courtier.*

Old Elizabethan Song.

Old Grimes ◡ ◡ ◡ ◡

OLD Grimes is dead; that good old man
    We never shall see more:
He used to wear a long, black coat,
    All button'd down before.

His heart was open as the day,
    His feelings all were true;
His hair was some inclined to gray—
    He wore it in a queue.

Whene'er he heard the voice of pain,
    His breast with pity burn'd;
The large round head upon his cane
    From ivory was turn'd.

* Other lines omitted. See note, p. 343.

Kind words he ever had for all ;
    He knew no base design :
His eyes were dark and rather small,
    His nose was aquiline.

He lived at peace with all mankind,
    In friendship he was true :
His coat had pocket-holes behind,
    His pantaloons were blue.

Unharm'd, the sin which earth pollutes
    He pass'd securely o'er,
And never wore a pair of boots
    For thirty years or more.

But good old Grimes is now at rest,
    Nor fears misfortune's frown :
He wore a double-breasted vest—
    The stripes ran up and down.

He modest merit sought to find,
    And pay it its desert :
He had no malice in his mind,
    No ruffles on his shirt.

His neighbours he did not abuse—
    Was sociable and gay :
He wore large buckles on his shoes,
    And changed them every day.

His knowledge, hid from public gaze,
    He did not bring to view,
Nor make a noise, town-meeting days,
    As many people do.

His worldly goods he never threw
   In trust to fortune's chances,
But lived (as all his brothers do)
   In easy circumstances.

Thus undisturb'd by anxious cares,
   His peaceful moments ran ;
And everybody said he was
   A fine old gentleman.

Albert G. Greene.

Tom Moody ⌀ ⌀ ⌀ ⌀ ⌀

YOU all knew Tom Moody, the whipper-in, well ;
   The bell just done tolling was honest Tom's knell ;
A more able sportsman ne'er followed a hound,
Through a country well known to him fifty miles round.
No hound ever open'd, with Tom near the wood,
But he'd challenge the tone, and could tell if 'twere good ;
And all with attention would eagerly mark,
When he cheered up the pack, " Hark, to Rockwood, hark !
    hark !
High !—wind him ! and cross him !
Now, Rattler, boy !—Hark ! "

Six crafty earth-stoppers, in hunter's green drest,
Supported poor Tom to "an earth " made for rest :
His horse, which he styled his " Old Soul," next appear'd,
On whose forehead the brush of his last fox was rear'd ;
Whip, cap, boots, and spurs in a trophy were bound,
And here and there follow'd an old straggling hound.

Ah! no more at his voice yonder vales will they trace!
Nor the welkin resound his burst in the chase!
With "High over!—Now press him!
Tally ho!—Tally ho!"

Thus Tom spoke his friends, ere he gave up his breath:
"Since I see you've resolved to be in at the death,
One favour bestow—'tis the last I shall crave,
Give a rattling view-halloo thrice over my grave;
And unless at that warning I lift up my head,
My boys, you may fairly conclude I am dead!"
Honest Tom was obey'd, and the shout rent the sky,
For ev'ry voice joined in the tally ho cry,
" Tally ho!   Hark forward!
Tally ho!—Tally ho!"

Anon.

A Dutch Picture

SIMON DANZ has come home again,
   From cruising about with his buccaneers;
He has singed the beard of the King of Spain,
And carried away the Dean of Jaen
   And sold him in Algiers.

In his house by the Maese, with its roof of tiles,
   And weathercocks flying aloft in air,
There are silver tankards of antique styles,
Plunder of convent and castle, and piles
   Of carpets rich and rare.

In his tulip-garden there by the town,
    Overlooking the sluggish stream,
With his Moorish cap and dressing-gown,
The old sea-captain, hale and brown,
    Walks in a waking dream.

A smile in his gray mustachio lurks
    Whenever he thinks of the King of Spain,
And the listed tulips look like Turks,
And the silent gardener as he works
    Is changed to the Dean of Jaen.

The windmills on the outermost
    Verge of the landscape in the haze,
To him are towers on the Spanish coast,
With whiskered sentinels at their post,
    Though this is the river Maese.

But when the winter rains begin,
    He sits and smokes by the blazing brands,
And old seafaring men come in,
Goat-bearded, gray, and with double chin,
    And rings upon their hands.

They sit there in the shadow and shine
    Of the flickering fire of the winter night;
Figures in colour and design
Like those by Rembrandt of the Rhine,
    Half darkness and half light.

And they talk of ventures lost or won,
    And their talk is ever and ever the same,

While they drink the red wine of Tarragon,
From the cellars of some Spanish Don,
   Or convent set on flame.

Restless at times with heavy strides
   He paces his parlour to and fro ;
He is like a ship that at anchor rides,
And swings with the rising and falling tides,
   And tugs at her anchor-tow.

Voices mysterious far and near,
   Sound of the wind and sound of the sea,
Are calling and whispering in his ear,
"Simon Danz ! Why stayest thou here?
   Come forth and follow me ! "

So he thinks he shall take to the sea again
   For one more cruise with his buccaneers,
To singe the beard of the King of Spain,
And capture another Dean of Jaen
   And sell him in Algiers.

H. W. Longfellow

THE SEA AND
THE ISLAND

Ye Mariners of England ❀

YE mariners of England!
   That guard our native seas;
Whose flag has braved, a thousand years.
   The battle and the breeze!
Your glorious standard launch again
   To match another foe!
And sweep through the deep,
   While the stormy winds do blow;
While the battle rages loud and long,
   And the stormy winds do blow.

The spirits of your fathers
   Shall start from every wave!
For the deck it was their field of fame,
   And ocean was their grave;
Where Blake and mighty Nelson fell,
   Your manly hearts shall glow,
As ye sweep through the deep,
   While the stormy winds do blow;
While the battle rages loud and long,
   And the stormy winds do blow.

Britannia needs no bulwarks,
   No towers along the steep;

Her march is o'er the mountain-waves,
  Her home is on the deep !
With thunders from her native oak,
  She quells the floods below,
As they roar on the shore,
  When the stormy winds do blow;
When the battle rages loud and long,
  And the stormy winds do blow.

The meteor flag of England
  Shall yet terrific burn ;
Till danger's troubled night depart,
  And the star of peace return.
Then, then, ye ocean-warriors !
  Our song and feast shall flow
To the fame of your name,
  When the storm has ceased to blow;
When the fiery fight is heard no more,
  And the storm has ceased to blow.

Thomas Campbell.

The Sailor's Consolation   ∽

ONE night came on a hurricane,
  The sea was mountains rolling,
When Barney Buntline slewed his quid,
  And said to Billy Bowline :
"A strong nor'-wester's blowing, Bill,
  Hark ! don't ye hear it roar now !
Lord help 'em, how I pities them
  Unhappy folks on shore now.

"Foolhardy chaps as live in towns,
    What danger they are all in,
And now lie quaking in their beds,
    For fear the roof should fall in !
Poor creatures, how they envies us,
    And wishes, I've a notion,
For our good luck in such a storm,
    To be upon the ocean !

" And as for them that's out all day,
    On business from their houses,
And late at night returning home,
    To cheer their babes and spouses ;
While you and I, Bill, on the deck
    Are comfortably lying,
My eyes ! what tiles and chimney-pots
    About their heads are flying !

" Both you and I have oft-times heard
    How men are killed and undone,
By overturns from carriages,
    By thieves, and fires in London.
We know what risks these landsmen run,
    From noblemen to tailors ;
Then, Bill, let us thank Providence
    That you and I are sailors."

Charles Dibdin.

A Wet Sheet and a Flowing Sea

A WET sheet and a flowing sea,
   A wind that follows fast,
And fills the white and rustling sail,
   And bends the gallant mast;
And bends the gallant mast, my boys,
   While, like the eagle free,
Away the good ship flies, and leaves
   Old England on the lee.

"O for a soft and gentle wind!"
   I heard a fair one cry;
But give to me the snoring breeze,
   And white waves heaving high;
And white waves heaving high, my boys,
   The good ship tight and free—
The world of waters is our home,
   And merry men are we.

There's tempest in yon hornèd moon
   And lightning in yon cloud;
And hark the music, mariners—
   The wind is piping loud;
The wind is piping loud, my boys,
   The lightning flashing free—
While the hollow oak our palace is,
   Our heritage the sea.

Allan Cunningham.

The Crew of the Long Serpent ∾

(From *The Saga of King Olaf*)

SAFE at anchor in Drontheim bay
    King Olaf's fleet assembled lay,
  And, striped with white and blue,
Downward fluttered sail and banner,
As alights the screaming lanner;
Lustily cheered, in their wild manner,
  The Long Serpent's crew.

Her forecastle man was Ulf the Red;
Like a wolf's was his shaggy head,
  His teeth as large and white;
His beard, of gray and russet blended,
Round as a swallow's nest descended;
As standard-bearer he defended
  Olaf's flag in the fight.

Near him Kolbiorn had his place,
Like the King in garb and face,
  So gallant and so hale;
Every cabin-boy and varlet
Wondered at his cloak of scarlet;
Like a river, frozen and star-lit,
  Gleamed his coat of mail.

By the bulkhead, tall and dark,
Stood Thrand Rame of Thelemark,
  A figure gaunt and grand;
On his hairy arm imprinted
Was an anchor, azure-tinted;
Like Thor's hammer, huge and dinted
  Was his brawny hand.

R

Einar Tamberskelver, bare
To the winds his golden hair,
　　By the mainmast stood ;
Graceful was his form, and slender,
And his eyes were deep and tender
As a woman's, in the splendour
　　Of her maidenhood.

In the fore-hold Biorn and Bork
Watched the sailors at their work :
　　Heavens ! how they swore !
Thirty men they each commanded,
Iron-sinewed, horny-handed,
Shoulders broad, and chests expanded,
　　Tugging at the oar.

These, and many more like these,
With King Olaf sailed the seas,
　　Till the waters vast
Filled them with a vague devotion,
With the freedom and the motion,
With the roll and roar of ocean
　　And the sounding blast.

When they landed from the fleet,
How they roared through Drontheim's street,
　　Boisterous as the gale !
How they laughed and stamped and pounded,
Till the tavern roof resounded
And the host looked on astounded
　　As they drank the ale !

Never saw the wild North Sea
Such a gallant company
   Sail its billows blue !
Never, while they cruised and quarrelled,
Old King Gorm, or Blue-Tooth Harald,
Owned a ship so well apparelled,
   Boasted such a crew !

H. W. Longfellow.

The Captain stood on the Carronade   ∽   ∽

THE captain stood on the carronade—" First lieutenant,"
   says he,
"Send all my merry men aft here, for they must list to me :
I haven't the gift of the gab, my sons—because I'm bred
   to the sea,
That ship there is a Frenchman, who means to fight with
   we.
   Odds blood, hammer and tongs, long as I've been to
     sea,
   I've fought 'gainst every odds — but I've gained the
     victory.

"That ship there is a Frenchman, and if we don't take *she*,
'Tis a thousand bullets to one, that she will capture *we ;*
I haven't the gift of the gab, my boys, so each man to
   his gun,
If she's not mine in half-an-hour, I'll flog each mother's
   son.
   Odds bobs, hammer and tongs, long as I've been to sea,
   I've fought 'gainst every odds—and I've gained the
     victory."

We fought for twenty minutes, when the Frenchman had
    enough,
"I little thought," said he, "that your men were of such
    stuff."
The captain took the Frenchman's sword, a low bow made
    to he—
"I haven't the gift of the gab, Mounsieur, but polite I wish
    to be.
  Odds bobs, hammer and tongs, long as I've been to sea,
  I've fought 'gainst every odds—and I've gained the
    victory."

Our captain sent for all of us; "My merry men," said he,
" I haven't the gift of the gab, my lads, but yet I thankful be;
You've done your duty handsomely, each man stood to
    his gun,
If you hadn't, you villains, as sure as day, I'd have flogged
    each mother's son.
  Odds bobs, hammer and tongs, as long as I'm at sea,
  I'll fight 'gainst every odds—and I'll gain the victory."

Captain Marryat.

The Roast Beef of Old England   ᔐ   ᔐ

WHEN mighty roast beef was the Englishman's food,
    It ennobled our hearts, and enriched our blood;
Our soldiers were brave, and our courtiers were good.
  Oh, the roast beef of Old England!
  And oh, for Old England's roast beef!

But since we have learn'd from effeminate France
To eat their ragouts, as well as to dance,
We are fed up with nothing but vain complaisance.
  Oh, the roast beef of Old England!

Our fathers of old were robust, stout, and strong,
And kept open house, with good cheer all day long,
Which made their plump tenants rejoice in this song—
    Oh, the roast beef of Old England!

When good Queen Elizabeth sat on the throne,
Ere coffee and tea, and such slip-slops were known,
The world was in terror if e'en she did frown.
    Oh, the roast beef of Old England!

In *those* days, if fleets did presume on the main,
They seldom or never return'd back again;
As witness the vaunting Armada of Spain.
    Oh, the roast beef of Old England!

Oh, then we had stomachs to eat and to fight,
And when wrongs were cooking, to set ourselves right;
But now we're a—hm!—I could, but good-night.
    Oh, the roast beef of Old England,
    And oh, for Old England's roast beef!

                       R. Leveridge.

The British Grenadiers

SOME talk of Alexander, and some of Hercules;
    Of Hector and Lysander, and such great names as
       these;
But of all the world's brave heroes, there's none that can
    compare,
With a tow, row, row, row, row, row, to the British
    Grenadier.

Those heroes of antiquity ne'er saw a cannon ball,
Or knew the force of powder to slay their foes withal;

But our brave boys do know it, and banish all their fears,
Sing tow, row, row, row, row, row, for the British Grenadiers.

Whene'er we are commanded to storm the palisades,
Our leaders march with fusees, and we with hand grenades;
We throw them from the glacis, about the enemies' ears;
Sing tow, row, row, row, row, row, for the British Grenadiers.

And when the siege is over, we to the town repair,
The townsmen cry "Hurra, boys, here comes a grenadier,
Here come the grenadiers, my boys, who know no doubts
    or fears,
Then sing tow, row, row, row, row, row, for the British
    Grenadiers."

Then let us fill a bumper, and drink a health to those
Who carry cups and pouches, and wear the loupèd clothes;
May they and their commanders live happy all their years,
With a tow, row, row, row, row, row, for the British
    Grenadiers.

Old Song.

The War-song of Dinas Vawr ◡

THE mountain sheep are sweeter,
    But the valley sheep are fatter;
We therefore deemed it meeter
To carry off the latter.
We made an expedition;
We met a host, and quelled it;
We forced a strong position,
And killed the men who held it.

On Dyfed's richest valley,
Where herds of kine were browsing,

We made a mighty sally,
To furnish our carousing,
Fierce warriors rushed to meet us;
We met them, and o'erthrew them:
They struggled hard to beat us;
But we conquered them, and slew them.

As we drove our prize at leisure,
The king marched forth to catch us:
His rage surpassed all measure,
But his people could not match us.
He fled to his hall-pillars;
And, ere our force we led off,
Some sacked his house and cellars,
While others cut his head off.

We there, in strife bewild'ring,
Spilt blood enough to swim in:
We orphaned many children,
And widowed many women.
The eagles and the ravens
We glutted with our foemen;
The heroes and the cravens,
The spearmen and the bowmen.

We brought away from battle,
And much their land bemoaned them,
Two thousand head of cattle,
And the head of him who owned them:
Ednyfed, king of Dyfed,
His head was borne before us;
His wine and beasts supplied our feasts,
And his overthrow, our chorus.

T. L. Peacock.

The Song of the Western Men ⌣

A GOOD sword and a trusty hand,
   A merry heart and true,
King James's men shall understand
   What Cornish lads can do.

And have they fix'd the where and when?
   And shall Trelawney die?
Here's twenty thousand Cornishmen
   Will see the reason why!

Out spake their captain brave and bold,
   A merry wight was he:
"If London Tower were Michael's hold,
   We'll set Trelawney free!

We'll cross the Tamar, land to land,
   The Severn is no stay,—
All side by side and hand to hand,
   And who shall bid us nay?

And when we come to London wall,
   A pleasant sight to view,
Come forth, come forth, ye cowards all,
   To better men than you.

Trelawney he's in keep and hold,
   Trelawney he may die!
But here's twenty thousand Cornish bold,
   Will see the reason why!"

R. S. Hawker.

A BUNDLE OF STORIES

The Babes in the Wood ～

NOW ponder well, you parents deare,
    These wordes, which I shall write;
A doleful story you shall heare,
    In time brought forth to light.
A gentleman of good account
    In Norfolke dwelt of late,
Who did in honour far surmount
    Most men of his estate.

Sore sicke he was, and like to dye,
    No helpe his life could save;
His wife by him as sicke did lye,
    And both possest one grave.
No love between these two was lost,
    Each was to other kinde;
In love they liv'd, in love they dyed,
    And left two babes behinde:

The one a fine and pretty boy,
    Not passing three yeares olde;
The other a girl more young than he,
    And fram'd in beautyes molde.
The father left his little son,
    As plainly does appeare,

When he to perfect age should come,
  Three hundred poundes a yeare.

And to his little daughter Jane
  Five hundred poundes in gold,
To be paid downe on marriage-day,
  Which might not be controll'd:
But if the children chance to dye,
  Ere they to age should come,
Their uncle should possesse their wealth;
  For so the wille did run.

"Now, brother," said the dying man,
  "Look to my children deare;
Be good unto my boy and girl,
  No friendes else have they here:
To God and you I recommend
  My children deare this daye;
But little while be sure we have
  Within this world to staye.

"You must be father and mother both,
  And uncle all in one;
God knowes what will become of them,
  When I am dead and gone."
With that bespake their mother deare,
  "O brother kinde," quoth shee,
"You are the man must bring our babes
  To wealth or miserie:

"And if you keep them carefully,
  Then God will you reward;

But if you otherwise should deal,
    God will your deedes regard."
With lippes as cold as any stone,
    They kist their children small :
" God bless you both, my children deare " ;
    With that the teares did fall.

These speeches then their brother spake
    To this sicke couple there,
" The keeping of your little ones,
    Sweet sister, do not feare ;
God never prosper me nor mine,
    Nor aught else that I have,
If I do wrong your children deare,
    When you are layd in grave."

The parents being dead and gone,
    The children home he takes,
And bringes them straite into his house,
    Where much of them he makes.
He had not kept these pretty babes
    A twelvemonth and a daye,
But, for their wealth, he did devise
    To make them both awaye.

He bargain'd with two ruffians strong,
    Which were of furious mood,
That they should take these children young,
    And slaye them in a wood.
He told his wife an artful tale,
    He would the children send
To be brought up in faire Londòn,
    With one that was his friend.

Away then went these pretty babes,
  Rejoycing at that tide,
Rejoycing with a merrye minde,
  They should on cock-horse ride.
They prate and prattle pleasantly,
  As they rode on the waye,
To those that should their butchers be,
  And work their lives decaye :

So that the pretty speeche they had,
  Made Murder's heart relent ;
And they that undertooke the deed,
  Full sore did now repent.
Yet one of them more hard of heart,
  Did vowe to do his charge,
Because the wretch that hired him,
  Had paid him very large.

The other won't agree thereto,
  So here they fall to strife ;
With one another they did fight,
  About the children's life :
And he that was of mildest mood,
  Did slaye the other there,
Within an unfrequented wood ;
  The babes did quake for feare !

He took the children by the hand,
  Teares standing in their eye,
And bad them straitwaye follow him,
  And look they did not crye :
And two long miles he ledd them on,
  While they for food complaine :

"Staye here," quoth he, "I'll bring you bread,
  When I come backe againe."

These pretty babes, with hand in hand,
  Went wandering up and downe,
But never more could see the man
  Approaching from the town :
Their prettye lippes with black-berries
  Were all besmear'd and dyed,
And when they saw the darksome night,
  They sat them downe and cryed.

Thus wandered these poor innocents,
  Till deathe did end their grief,
In one another's armes they dyed,
  As wanting due relief :
No burial this pretty pair
  Of any man receives,
Till Robin-red-breast piously
  Did cover them with leaves.

And now the heavy wrathe of God
  Upon their uncle fell ;
Yea, fearfull fiends did haunt his house,
  His conscience felt an hell :
His barnes were fir'd, his goodes consum'd,
  His landes were barren made,
His cattle dyed within the field,
  And nothing with him stayd.

And in a voyage to Portugal
  Two of his sonnes did dye ;

And to conclude, himselfe was brought
    To want and miserye :
He pawn'd and mortgag'd all his land
    Ere seven yeares came about,
And now at length this wicked act
    Did by this meanes come out:

The fellowe, that did take in hand
    These children for to kill,
Was for a robbery judg'd to dye,
    Such was God's blessed will :
Who did confess the very truth
    As here hath been display'd :
Their uncle having dyed in gaol,
    Where he for debt was layd.

You that executors be made,
    And overseers eke
Of children that be fatherless,
    And infants mild and meek ;
Take you example by this thing,
    And yield to each his right,
Lest God with such like miserye
    Your wicked minds requite.

Old Ballad.

The Lady Isabella's Tragedy

THERE was a lord of worthy fame,
    And a-hunting he would ride,
Attended by a noble train
    Of gentrye by his side.

And while he did in chase remaine,
    To see both sport and playe ;
His ladye went, as she did feigne,
    Unto the church to praye.

This lord he had a daughter deare,
    Whose beauty shone so bright,
She was belov'd, both far and neare,
    Of many a lord and knight.

Fair Isabella was she call'd,
    A creature fair was shee ;
She was her father's only joye,
    As you shall after see.

Therefore her cruel step-mothèr
    Did envye her so much ;
That daye by daye she sought her life,
    Her malice it was such.

She bargain'd with the master-cook,
    To take her life awaye :
And, taking of her daughter's book,
    She thus to her did saye :

" Go home, sweet daughter, I thee praye,
    Go hasten presentlie ;
And tell unto the master-cook
    These wordes I tell thee.

" And bid him dresse to dinner streight
    That fair and milk-white doe,
That in the parke doth shine so bright,
    There's none so faire to showe."

S

This ladye, fearing of no harme,
   Obey'd her mother's will;
And presently she hasted home
   Her pleasure to fulfill.

She streight into the kitchen went,
   Her message for to tell;
And there she spied the master-cook,
   Who did with malice swell.

"Nowe, master-cook, it must be soe,
   Do that which I thee tell:
You needes must dress the milk-white doe,
   Which you do knowe full well."

Then streight his cruel bloodye hands
   He on the ladye layd;
Who quivering and shaking stands,
   While thus to her he sayd:

"Thou art the doe, that I must dress;
   See here, behold my knife;
For it is pointed presently
   To rid thee of thy life."

"O, then," cried out the scullion-boye,
   As loud as loud might bee;
"O save her life, good master-cook,
   And make your pyes of mee!

"For pityes sake do not destroye
   My ladye with your knife;
You know shee is her father's joye,
   For Christes sake save her life."

"I will not save her life," he sayd,
   "Nor make my pyes of thee ;
Yet if thou dost this deed bewraye,
   Thy butcher I will bee."

Now when this lord he did come home
   For to sit downe and eat ;
He callèd for his daughter deare,
   To come and carve his meat.

"Now sit you downe," his ladye said,
   "O sit you downe to meat :
Into some nunnery she is gone ;
   Your daughter deare forget."

Then solemnlye he made a vowe,
   Before the companiè :
That he would neither eat nor drinke,
   Until he did her see.

O then bespake the scullion-boye,
   With a loud voice so hye :
"If now you will your daughter see,
   My lord, cut up that pye :

"Wherein her fleshe is mincèd small,
   And parchèd with the fire ;
All caused by her step-mothèr,
   Who did her death desire.

"And cursed be the master-cook,
   O cursed may he bee !
I proffered him my own heart's blood
   From death to set her free."

Then all in black this lord did mourne;
   And for his daughter's sake,
He judged her cruell step-mothèr
   To be burnt at a stake.

Likewise he judg'd the master-cook
   In boiling lead to stand;
And made the simple scullion-boye
   The heire of all his land.

Old Ballad.

King Leir and His Three Daughters

KING LEIR once ruled in this land
   With princely power and peace;
And had all things with heart's content,
   That might his joys increase.
Amongst those things that nature gave,
   Three daughters fair had he,
So princely seeming, beautiful,
   As fairer could not be.

So on a time it pleas'd the king
   A question thus to move,
Which of his daughters to his grace
   Could shew the dearest love:
"For to my age you bring content,"
   Quoth he, "then let me hear,
Which of you three in plighted troth
   The kindest will appear."

To whom the eldest thus began :
  "Dear father, mind," quoth she,
"Before your face to do you good,
  My blood shall render'd be :
And for your sake my bleeding heart
  Shall here be cut in twain,
Ere that I see your reverend age
  The smallest grief sustain."

"And so will I," the second said,
  "Dear father, for your sake,
The worst of all extremities
  I'll gently undertake :
And serve your highness night and day
  With diligence and love ;
That sweet content and quietness
  Discomforts may remove."

"In doing so, you glad my soul,"
  The aged king reply'd ;
"But what sayst thou, my youngest girl,
  How is thy love ally'd ?"
"My love" (quoth young Cordelia then)
  "Which to your Grace I owe,
Shall be the duty of a child,
  And that is all I'll show."

"And wilt thou show no more," quoth he,
  "Than doth thy duty bind ?
I well perceive thy love is small,
  When as no more I find.
Henceforth I banish thee my court,
  Thou art no child of mine ;

Nor any part of this my realm
  By favour shall be thine.

"Thy elder sisters' loves are more
  Than I can well demand,
To whom I equally bestow
  My kingdome and my land,
My pompal state and all my goods,
  That lovingly I may
With those thy sisters be maintain'd
  Until my dying day."

Thus flattering speeches won renown
  By these two sisters here;
The third had causeless banishment,
  Yet was her love more dear:
For poor Cordelia patiently
  Went wand'ring up and down,
Unhelp'd, unpity'd, gentle maid,
  Through many an English town.

Untill at last in famous France
  She gentler fortunes found;
Though poor and bare, yet she was deem'd
  The fairest on the ground:
Where when the king her virtues heard,
  And this fair lady seen,
With full consent of all his court,
  He made his wife and queen.

Her father King Leir this while
  With his two daughters staid:
Forgetful of their promis'd loves,
  Full soon the same decay'd;

And living in Queen Ragan's court,
   The eldest of the twain,
She took from him his chiefest means,
   And most of all his train.

For whereas twenty men were wont
   To wait with bended knee,
She gave allowance but to ten,
   And after scarce to three;
Nay, one she thought too much for him;
   So took she all away,
In hope that in her court, good king,
   He would no longer stay.

"Am I rewarded thus," quoth he,
   "In giving all I have
Unto my children, and to beg
   For what I lately gave?
I'll go unto my Gonorell:
   My second child, I know,
Will be more kind and pitiful,
   And will relieve my woe."

Full fast he hies then to her court;
   Where when she heard his moan
Return'd him answer, That she griev'd
   That all his means were gone:
But no way could relieve his wants;
   Yet, if that he would stay
Within her kitchen, he should have
   What scullions gave away.

When he had heard, with bitter tears,
   He made his answer then;

"In what I did, let me be made
Example to all men.
I will return again," quoth he,
"Unto my Ragan's court;
She will not use me thus, I hope,
But in a kinder sort."

Where when he came, she gave command
To drive him thence away:
When he was well within her court
(She said) he would not stay.
Then back to Gonorell,
The woful king did hie,
That in her kitchen he might have
What scullion boys set by.

But there of that he was deny'd,
Which she had promised late:
For once refusing, he should not
Come after to her gate.
Thus twixt his daughters, for relief
He wand'red up and down;
Being glad to feed on beggar's food,
That lately wore a crown.

And calling to remembrance then
His youngest daughter's words,
That said the duty of a child
Was all that love affords:
But doubting to repair to her,
Whom he had banish'd so,
Grew frantick mad; for in his mind
He bore the wounds of woe:

Which made him rend his milk-white locks
    And tresses from his head,
And all with blood bestain his cheeks,
    With age and honour spread.
To hills and woods and wat'ry founts
    He made his hourly moan,
Till hills and woods and sensless things
    Did seem to sigh and groan.

Even thus possest with discontents,
    He passèd o'er to France,
In hopes from fair Cordelia there,
    To find some gentler chance;
Most virtuous dame! which when she heard
    Of this her father's grief,
As duty bound, she quickly sent
    Him comfort and relief:

And by a train of noble peers,
    In brave and gallant sort,
She gave in charge he should be brought
    To Aganippus' court;
Whose royal king, with noble mind
    So freely gave consent,
To muster up his knights at arms
    To fame and courage bent.

And so to England came with speed,
    To repossesse King Leir,
And drive his daughters from their thrones
    By his Cordelia dear.
Where she, true-hearted noble queen,
    Was in the battel slain:

Yet he good king, in his old days,
　　Possest his crown again.

But when he heard Cordelia's death,
　　Who died indeed for love
Of her dear father, in whose cause
　　She did this battle move;
He swooning fell upon her breast,
　　From whence he never parted:
But on her bosom left his life,
　　That was so truly hearted.

The lords and nobles when they saw
　　The end of these events,
The other sisters unto death
　　They doomèd by consents;
And being dead, their crowns they left
　　Unto the next of kin:
Thus have you seen the fall of pride,
　　And disobedient sin.

　　　　　　　　　　　　　Old Ballad.

King John and the Abbot of Canterbury　∿

AN ancient story Ile tell you anon
　　Of a notable prince, that was called King John;
And he ruled England with maine and with might,
For he did great wrong and maintein'd little right.

And Ile tell you a story, a story so merrye,
Concerning the Abbot of Canterburye;
How for his house-keeping and high renowne,
They rode poste for him to fair London towne.

An hundred men, the king did heare say,
The Abbot kept in his house every day;
And fifty golde chaynes, without any doubt,
In velvet coates waited the Abbot about.

"How now, father abbot, I heare it of thee,
Thou keepest a farre better house than mee,
And for thy house-keeping and high renowne,
I fear thou work'st treason against my crown."

"My liege," quo' the abbot, "I would it were knowne,
I never spend nothing, but what is my owne;
And I trust, your grace will do me no deere *
For spending of my owne true-gotten geere."

"Yes, yes, father abbot, thy fault it is highe,
And now for the same thou needest must dye;
For except thou canst answer me questions three,
Thy head shall be smitten from thy bodie.

"And first," quo' the king, "when I'm in this stead,
With my crown of golde so faire on my head,
Among all my liege-men so noble of birthe,
Thou must tell me to one penny what I am worthe.

"Secondlye tell me, without any doubt,
How soon I may ride the whole worlde about.
And at the third question thou must not shrink,
But tell me here truly what I do think."

* Harm.

" O, these are hard questions for my shallow witt,
Nor I cannot answer your grace as yet ;
But if you will give me but three weekes space,
Ile do my endeavour to answer your grace."

" Now three weeks' space to thee will I give,
And that is the longest time thou hast to live ;
For if thou dost not answer my questions three,
Thy lands and thy living are forfeit to mee."

Away rode the abbot all sad at that word,
And he rode to Cambridge, and Oxenford ;
But never a doctor there was so wise,
That could with his learning an answer devise.

Then home rode the abbot of comfort so cold,
And he mett his shephard a-going to fold :
" How now, my lord abbot, you are welcome home ;
What newes do you bring us from good King John ? "

" Sad newes, sad newes, shephard, I must give ;
That I have but three days more to live :
For if I do not answer him questions three,
My head will be smitten from my bodie.

" The first is to tell him there in that stead,
With his crowne of golde so faire on his head,
Among all his liegemen so noble of birth,
To within one penny of what he is worth.

" The seconde, to tell him without any doubt,
How soon he may ride this whole world about :
And at the third question I must not shrinke,
But tell him there truly what he does thinke."

"Now cheare up, sire abbot, did you never hear yet
That a fool he may learn a wise man witt?
Lend me horse, and serving-men, and your apparel,
And I'll ride to London to answere your quarrel.

"Nay frowne not, if it hath bin told unto mee,
I am like your lordship, as ever may bee;
And if you will but lend me your gowne:
There is none shall knowe us at fair London towne."

"Now horses, and serving-men thou shalt have,
With sumptuous array most gallant and brave;
With crozier, and miter, and rochet, and cope,
Fit to appeare 'fore our fader the pope."

"Now welcome, sire abbot," the King he did say,
"'Tis well thou'rt come back to keepe thy day:
For and if thou canst answer my questions three,
Thy life and thy living both saved shall bee."

"And first, when thou see'st me here in this stead,
With my crown of golde so fair on my head,
Among all my liege-men so noble of birthe,
Tell me to one penny what I am worth."

"For thirty pence our Saviour was sold
Amonge the false Jewes, as I have bin told:
And twenty-nine is the worth of thee,
For I thinke, thou art one penny worser than Hee."

The king he laugh'd, and swore by St. Bittel,
"I did not think I had been worth so littel!
—Now secondly, tell me, without any doubt,
How soone I may ride this whole world about."

"You must rise with the sun, and ride with the same,
Until the next morning he riseth againe;
And then your grace need not make any doubt,
But in twenty-four hours you'll ride it about."

The king he laugh'd, and swore by St. Jone,
"I did not think it could be done so soone!
—Now from the third question you must not shrinke,
But tell me here truly what I do thinke."

"Yea, that shall I do and make your grace merry:
You thinke I'm the abbot of Canterbury;
But I'm his poor shephard, as plain you may see,
That am come to beg pardon for him and for mee."

The King he laughed, and swore by the masse,
"Ile make thee lord abbot this day in his place!"
"Now nay, my liege, be not in such speede,
For alacke I can neither write, ne reade."

"Four nobles a weeke, then, I will give thee,
For this merry jest thou hast showne unto me;
And tell the old abbot, when thou comest home,
Thou hast brought him a pardon from good King John."

Old Ballad.

The Glove and the Lions   ∽   ∽   ∽   ∽

KING FRANCIS was a hearty king, and lov'd a royal
    sport,
And one day, as his lions fought, sat looking on the court;
The nobles fill'd the benches, and the ladies in their pride,

And 'mongst them sat the Count de Lorge, with one for
    whom he sigh'd :
And truly 'twas a gallant thing to see that crowning show,
Valour and love, and a king above, and the royal beasts
    below.

Ramp'd and roar'd the lions, with horrid laughing jaws ;
They bit, they glared, gave blows like beams, a wind went
    with their paws ;
With wallowing might and stifled roar they roll'd on one
    another,
Till all the pit with sand and mane was in a thunderous
    smother ;
The bloody foam above the bars came whisking through
    the air ;
Said Francis then, "Faith, gentlemen, we're better here
    than there."

De Lorge's love o'erheard the King, a beauteous lively
    dame,
With smiling lips and sharp bright eyes, which always
    seem'd the same ;
She thought, "The Count my lover is brave as brave can
    be ;
He surely would do wondrous things to show his love of
    me ;
King, ladies, lovers, all look on ; the occasion is divine ;
I'll drop my glove to prove his love ; great glory will be
    mine."

She dropp'd her glove to prove his love, then look'd at
    him and smil'd ;
He bow'd, and in a moment leap'd among the lions wild :

The leap was quick, return was quick, he has regain'd the
place,
Then threw the glove, but not with love, right in the lady's
face.
"My faith!" said Francis, "rightly done!" and he rose
from where he sat ;
"No love," quoth he, " but vanity, sets love a task like that."

Leigh Hunt.

The Fakenham Ghost ∽ ∽

THE lawns were dry in Euston park
   (Here truth inspires my tale).
The lonely footpath, still and dark,
   Led over hill and dale.

Benighted was an ancient dame,
   And fearful haste she made
To join the Vale of Fakenham,
   And hail its willow shade.

Her footsteps knew no idle stops,
   But followed faster still ;
And echoed to the darksome copse
   That whispered on the hill.

Where clamorous rooks, yet scarcely hushed,
   Bespoke a peopled shade ;
And many a wing the foliage brushed
   And hovering circuits made.

The dappled herd of grazing deer,
  That sought the shades by day,
Now started from her path with fear,
  And gave the stranger way.

Darker it grew, and darker fears
  Came o'er the troubled mind;
When now, a short quick step she hears
  Come patting close behind.

She turned—it stopt—nought could she see
  Upon the gloomy plain!
But, as she strove the Sprite to flee,
  She heard the same again.

Now terror seized her quaking frame;
  For, where the path was bare,
The trotting ghost kept on the same!
  She muttered many a prayer.

Yet once again, amidst her fright,
  She tried what sight could do;
When, through the cheating gloom of night,
  A monster stood in view.

Regardless of whate'er she felt,
  It followed down the plain!
She owned her sins, and down she knelt,
  And said her prayers again.

Then on she sped, and hope grew strong,
  The white park-gate in view;
Which pushing hard, so long it swung,
  That ghost and all passed through.

T

Loud fell the gate against the post !
  Her heart-strings like to crack :
For much she feared the grizzly ghost
  Would leap upon her back.

Still on, pat, pat, the goblin went,
  As it had done before—
Her strength and resolution spent,
  She fainted at the door.

Out came her husband, much surprised ;
  Out came her daughter dear ;
Good-natured souls ! all unadvised
  Of what they had to fear.

The candle's gleam pierced through the night
  Some short space o'er the green ;
And there the little trotting Sprite
  Distinctly might be seen.

An ass's foal had lost its dam
  Within the spacious park ;
And, simple as the playful lamb,
  Had followed in the dark.

No Goblin he ; no imp of sin ;
  No crimes had e'er he known ;
They took the shaggy stranger in,
  And reared him as their own.

His little hoofs would rattle round
  Upon the cottage floor ;
The matron learned to love the sound
  That frightened her before.

A favourite the Ghost became,
    And 'twas his fate to thrive;
And long he lived, and spread his fame,
    And kept the joke alive.

For many a laugh went through the vale,
    And some conviction too;
Each thought some other goblin tale,
    Perhaps was just as true.

Robert Bloomfield.

Bishop Hatto ❧ ❧ ❧ ❧

THE summer and autumn had been so wet
    That in winter the corn was growing yet;
'Twas a piteous sight to see all around
The corn lie rotting on the ground.

Every day the starving poor
They crowded around Bishop Hatto's door,
For he had a plentiful last-year's store,
And all the neighbourhood could tell
His granaries were furnished well.

At last Bishop Hatto appointed a day
To quiet the poor without delay;
He bade them to his great barn repair,
And they should have food for the winter there.

Rejoiced such tidings good to hear,
The poor folk flock'd from far and near;
The great barn was full as it could hold
Of women and children, and young and old.

Then when he saw it could hold no more,
Bishop Hatto he made fast the door;
And whilst for mercy on Christ they call,
He set fire to the barn and burnt them all.

"I' faith, 'tis an excellent bonfire!" quoth he,
"And the country is greatly obliged to me,
For ridding it in these times forlorn,
Of rats that only consume the corn."

So then to his palace returnèd he,
And he sat down to supper merrily,
And he slept that night like an innocent man,
But Bishop Hatto never slept again.

In the morning as he enter'd the hall,
Where his picture hung against the wall,
A sweat like death all over him came,
For the rats had eaten it out of the frame.

As he look'd there came a man from his farm,
He had a countenance white with alarm;
"My lord, I open'd your granaries this morn,
And the rats had eaten all your corn."

Another came running presently,
And he was pale as pale could be,
"Fly! my Lord Bishop, fly!" quoth he,

"Ten thousand rats are coming this way—
The Lord forgive you for yesterday!"

"I'll go to my tower in the Rhine," replied he,
"'Tis the safest place in Germany;
The walls are high, and the shores are steep,
And the tide is strong, and the water deep."

Bishop Hatto fearfully hasten'd away,
And he cross'd the Rhine without delay,
And reach'd his tower in the island and barr'd
All the gates secure and hard.

He laid him down and closed his eyes—
But soon a scream made him arise;
He started, and saw two eyes of flame
On his pillow from whence the screaming came.

He listen'd and look'd;—it was only the cat;
But the Bishop he grew more fearful for that,
For she sat screaming, mad with fear,
At the army of rats that were drawing near.

For they have swum over the river so deep,
And they have climb'd the shores so steep,
And now by thousands up they crawl
To the holes and the windows in the wall.

Down on his knees the Bishop fell,
And faster and faster his beads did he tell,
As louder and louder drawing near
The saw of their teeth without he could hear.

And in at the windows, and in at the door,
And through the walls by thousands they pour,
And down from the ceiling, and up through the floor,
From the right and the left, from behind and before,
From within and without, from above and below,
And all at once to the Bishop they go.

They have whetted their teeth against the stones,
And now they pick the Bishop's bones ;
They gnaw'd the flesh from every limb,
For they were sent to do judgment on him !

Robert Southey.

The Diverting History of John Gilpin; showing how he went farther than he intended, and came safe home again ∾

JOHN GILPIN was a citizen
   Of credit and renown,
A train-band captain eke was he
   Of famous London town.

John Gilpin's spouse said to her dear,
   "Though wedded we have been
These twice ten tedious years, yet we
   No holiday have seen.

"To-morrow is our wedding day
   And we will then repair
Unto the Bell at Edmonton
   All in a chaise and pair.

"My sister, and my sister's child,
   Myself and children three,
Will fill the chaise; so you must ride
   On horseback after we."

He soon replied, "I do admire
   Of womankind but one,
And you are she, my dearest dear,
   Therefore it shall be done.

"I am a linen-draper bold,
   As all the world doth know,
And my good friend the Calender
   Will lend his horse to go."

Quoth Mrs. Gilpin, "That's well said;
   And for that wine is dear,
We will be furnished with our own,
   Which is both bright and clear."

John Gilpin kissed his loving wife;
   O'erjoyed was he to find
That, though on pleasure she was bent,
   She had a frugal mind.

The morning came, the chaise was brought,
   But yet was not allow'd
To drive up to the door, lest all
   Should say that she was proud.

So three doors off the chaise was stayed,
   Where they did all get in;
Six precious souls, and all agog
   To dash through thick and thin.

Smack went the whip, round went the wheels,
    Were never folk so glad,
The stones did rattle underneath,
    As if Cheapside were mad.

John Gilpin at his horse's side
    Seiz'd fast the flowing mane,
And up he got, in haste to ride,
    But soon came down again;

For saddle-tree scarce reached had he,
    His journey to begin,
When, turning round his head, he saw
    Three customers come in.

So down he came; for loss of time,
    Although it grieved him sore,
Yet loss of pence, full well he knew,
    Would trouble him much more.

'Twas long before the customers
    Were suited to their mind,
When Betty screaming came down stairs,
    "The wine is left behind!"

"Good lack," quoth he,—"yet bring it me,
    My leathern belt likewise,
In which I bear my trusty sword
    When I do exercise."

Now Mistress Gilpin (careful soul!)
    Had two stone bottles found,
To hold the liquor that she loved,
    And keep it safe and sound.

Each bottle had a curling ear,
　　Through which the belt he drew,
And hung a bottle on each side,
　　To make his balance true.

Then over all, that he might be
　　Equipp'd from top to toe,
His long red cloak, well brush'd and neat,
　　He manfully did throw.

Now see him mounted once again
　　Upon his nimble steed,
Full slowly pacing o'er the stones
　　With caution and good heed.

But finding soon a smoother road
　　Beneath his well-shod feet,
The snorting beast began to trot,
　　Which galled him in his seat.

So, "Fair and softly," John he cried,
　　But John he cried in vain;
That trot became a gallop soon,
　　In spite of curb and rein.

So stooping down, as needs he must
　　Who cannot sit upright,
He grasp'd the mane with both his hands,
　　And eke with all his might.

His horse, who never in that sort
　　Had handled been before,
What thing upon his back had got
　　Did wonder more and more.

Away went Gilpin, neck or nought;
    Away went hat and wig;
He little dreamt, when he set out,
    Of running such a rig.

The wind did blow, the cloak did fly.
    Like streamer long and gay,
Till, loop and button failing both,
    At last it flew away.

Then might all people well discern
    The bottles he had slung;
A bottle swinging at each side,
    As hath been said or sung.

The dogs did bark, the children scream'd,
    Up flew the windows all;
And every soul cried out, " Well done !"
    As loud as he could bawl.

Away went Gilpin—who but he ?
    His fame soon spread around;
" He carries weight ! he rides a race !
    'Tis for a thousand pound ! "

And still, as fast as he drew near,
    'Twas wonderful to view,
How in a trice the turnpike-men
    Their gates wide open threw.

And now, as he went bowing down
    His reeking head full low,
The bottles twain behind his back
    Were shatter'd at a blow.

Down ran the wine into the road,
    Most piteous to be seen,
Which made his horse's flanks to smoke
    As they had basted been.

But still he seem'd to carry weight,
    With leathern girdle braced;
For all might see the bottle necks
    Still dangling at his waist.

Thus all through merry Islington
    These gambols he did play,
Until he came unto the Wash
    Of Edmonton so gay;

And there he threw the Wash about
    On both sides of the way,
Just like unto a trundling mop,
    Or a wild goose at play.

At Edmonton his loving wife
    From the balcony spied
Her tender husband, wond'ring much
    To see how he did ride.

"Stop, stop, John Gilpin!—Here's the house—"
    They all aloud did cry;
"The dinner waits, and we are tired":
    Said Gilpin—"So am I!"

But yet his horse was not a whit
    Inclin'd to tarry there;
For why?—his owner had a house
    Full ten miles off, at Ware.

So like an arrow swift he flew,
  Shot by an archer strong ;
So did he fly—which brings me to
  The middle of my song.

Away went Gilpin out of breath,
  And sore against his will,
Till at his friend the Calender's
  His horse at last stood still.

The Calender, amazed to see
  His neighbour in such trim,
Laid down his pipe, flew to the gate,
  And thus accosted him :

" What news ? what news ? your tidings tell ;
  Tell me you must and shall—
Say why bare-headed you are come,
  Or why you come at all ? "

Now Gilpin had a pleasant wit,
  And loved a timely joke :
And thus unto the Calender
  In merry guise he spoke :

" I came because your horse would come ;
  And, if I well forbode,
My hat and wig will soon be here,
  They are upon the road."

The Calender, right glad to find
  His friend in merry pin,
Return'd him not a single word,
  But to the house went in ;

Whence straight he came with hat and wig;
   A wig that flowed behind,
A hat not much the worse for wear,
   Each comely in its kind.

He held them up, and in his turn
   Thus show'd his ready wit :
" My head is twice as big as yours,
   They therefore needs must fit.

" But let me scrape the dirt away,
   That hangs upon your face ;
And stop and eat, for well you may
   Be in a hungry case."

Said John, " It is my wedding-day,
   And all the world would stare,
If wife should dine at Edmonton,
   And I should dine at Ware."

So turning to his horse, he said,
   " I am in haste to dine ;
'Twas for your pleasure you came here,
   You shall go back for mine."

Ah, luckless speech, and bootless boast
   For which he paid full dear ;
For, while he spake, a braying ass
   Did sing most loud and clear ;

Whereat his horse did snort, as he
   Had heard a lion roar,
And galloped off with all his might,
   As he had done before.

Away went Gilpin, and away
    Went Gilpin's hat and wig:
He lost them sooner than at first,
    For why?—they were too big.

Now Mistress Gilpin, when she saw
    Her husband posting down
Into the country far away,
    She pulled out half-a-crown;

And thus unto the youth she said,
    That drove them to the Bell:
" This shall be yours, when you bring back
    My husband safe and well."

The youth did ride, and soon did meet
    John coming back amain!
Whom in a trice he tried to stop,
    By catching at his rein;

But not performing what he meant,
    And gladly would have done,
The frighted steed he frighted more,
    And made him faster run.

Away went Gilpin, and away
    Went post-boy at his heels,
The post-boy's horse right glad to miss
    The lumb'ring of the wheels.

Six gentlemen upon the road
    Thus seeing Gilpin fly,
With post-boy scampering in the rear.
    They raised the hue-and-cry:—

"Stop thief! stop thief!—a highwayman!"
   Not one of them was mute;
And all and each that passed that way
   Did join in the pursuit.

And now the turnpike gates again
   Flew open in short space;
The toll-men thinking as before,
   That Gilpin rode a race.

And so he did, and won it too,
   For he got first to town;
Nor stopped till where he had got up
   He did again get down.

Now let us sing, long live the King,
   And Gilpin, long live he;
And, when he next doth ride abroad,
   May I be there to see!

                              William Cowper.

The Pied Piper of Hamelin   ◞   ◞

I

HAMELIN Town's in Brunswick,
   By famous Hanover city;
The river Weser, deep and wide,
Washes its wall on the southern side;
A pleasanter spot you never spied;
   But, when begins my ditty,

Almost five hundred years ago,
To see the townsfolk suffer so
  From vermin, was a pity.

II

  Rats!
They fought the dogs, and killed the cats,
  And bit the babies in the cradles,
And ate the cheeses out of the vats,
  And licked the soup from the cook's own ladles,
Split open the kegs of salted sprats,
Made nests inside men's Sunday hats,
And even spoiled the women's chats,
  By drowning their speaking
  With shrieking and squeaking
In fifty different sharps and flats.

III

At last the people in a body
  To the Town Hall came flocking:
" 'Tis clear," cried they, " our Mayor's a noddy;
  And as for our Corporation—shocking
To think we buy gowns lined with ermine
For dolts that can't or won't determine
What's best to rid us of our vermin!
You hope, because you're old and obese,
To find in the furry civic robe ease?
Rouse up, sirs! Give your brains a racking
To find the remedy we're lacking,
Or, sure as fate, we'll send you packing!"
At this the Mayor and Corporation
Quaked with a mighty consternation.

IV

An hour they sate in council,
    At length the Mayor broke silence:
"For a guilder I'd my ermine gown sell;
    I wish I were a mile hence!
It's easy to bid one rack one's brain—
I'm sure my poor head aches again
I've scratched it so, and all in vain.
Oh for a trap, a trap, a trap!"
Just as he said this, what should hap
At the chamber door but a gentle tap?
"Bless us," cried the Mayor, "what's that?"
(With the Corporation as he sat,
Looking little though wondrous fat;
Nor brighter was his eye, nor moister
Than a too-long-opened oyster,
Save when at noon his paunch grew mutinous
For a plate of turtle green and glutinous)
"Only a scraping of shoes on the mat?
Anything like the sound of a rat
Makes my heart go pit-a-pat!"

V

"Come in!"—the Mayor cried, looking bigger:
And in did come the strangest figure!
His queer long coat from heel to head
Was half of yellow and half of red,
And he himself was tall and thin,
With sharp blue eyes, each like a pin,
And light loose hair, yet swarthy skin,
No tuft on cheek nor beard on chin,
But lips where smiles went out and in;

U

There was no guessing his kith and kin:
And nobody could enough admire
The tall man and his quaint attire.
Quoth one: "It's as my great-grandsire,
Starting up at the Trump of Doom's tone,
Had walked this way from his painted tombstone!"

VI

He advanced to the council-table:
And, "Please your honours," said he, "I'm able,
By means of a secret charm, to draw
    All creatures living beneath the sun,
    That creep or swim or fly or run,
After me so as you never saw!
And I chiefly use my charm
On creatures that do people harm,
The mole and toad and newt and viper;
And people call me the Pied Piper."
(And here they noticed round his neck
    A scarf of red and yellow stripe,
To match with his coat of the self-same check;
    And at the scarf's end hung a pipe;
And his fingers, they noticed, were ever straying
As if impatient to be playing
Upon this pipe, as low it dangled
Over his vesture so old-fangled.)
"Yet," said he, "poor piper as I am,
In Tartary I freed the Cham,
    Last June, from his huge swarm of gnats;
I eased in Asia the Nizam
    Of a monstrous brood of vampyre-bats:
And as for what your brain bewilders,

If I can rid your town of rats
Will you give me a thousand guilders?"
" One? fifty thousand!"—was the exclamation
Of the astonished Mayor and Corporation.

VII

Into the street the Piper stept,
 Smiling first a little smile,
As if he knew what magic slept
 In his quiet pipe the while;
Then, like a musical adept,
To blow the pipe his lips he wrinkled,
And green and blue his sharp eyes twinkled
Like a candle flame where salt is sprinkled;
And ere three shrill notes the pipe uttered,
You heard as if an army muttered;
And the muttering grew to a grumbling;
And the grumbling grew to a mighty rumbling;
And out of the houses the rats came tumbling.
Great rats, small rats, lean rats, brawny rats,
Brown rats, black rats, grey rats, tawny rats,
Grave old plodders, gay young friskers,
 Fathers, mothers, uncles, cousins,
Cocking tails and pricking whiskers,
 Families by tens and dozens,
Brothers, sisters, husbands, wives—
Followed the Piper for their lives.
From street to street he piped advancing,
And step for step they followed dancing,
Until they came to the river Weser,
 Wherein all plunged and perished:
— Save one who, stout as Julius Cæsar,

Swam across and lived to carry
   (As he, the manuscript he cherished)
To Rat-land home his commentary:
Which was, "At the first shrill notes of the pipe,
I heard a sound as of scraping tripe,
And putting apples, wondrous ripe,
Into a cider-press's gripe:
And a moving away of pickle-tub-boards,
And a leaving ajar of conserve-cupboards,
And a drawing the corks of train-oil-flasks,
And a breaking the hoops of butter-casks:
And it seemed as if a voice
   (Sweeter far than by harp or by psaltery
Is breathed) called out, 'Oh rats, rejoice!
   The world is grown to one vast drysaltery!
So munch on, crunch on, take your nuncheon,
Breakfast, supper, dinner, luncheon!'
And just as a bulky sugar-puncheon,
All ready staved, like a great sun shone
Glorious scarce an inch before me,
Just as methought it said, 'Come, bore me!'
—I found the Weser rolling o'er me."

VIII

You should have heard the Hamelin people
Ringing the bells till they rocked the steeple;
"Go," cried the Mayor, "and get long poles!
Poke out the nests and block up the holes!
Consult with carpenters and builders,
And leave in our town not even a trace
Of the rats!"—when suddenly, up the face
Of the Piper perked in the market-place,
With a, "First, if you please, my thousand guilders!"

IX

A thousand guilders! The Mayor looked blue;
So did the Corporation too.
For council dinners made rare havock
With Claret, Moselle, Vin-de-Grave, Hock;
And half the money would replenish
Their cellar's biggest butt with Rhenish.
To pay this sum to a wandering fellow
With a gipsy coat of red and yellow!
"Beside," quoth the Mayor with a knowing wink,
"Our business was done at the river's brink;
We saw with our eyes the vermin sink,
And what's dead can't come to life, I think.
So, friend, we're not the folks to shrink
From the duty of giving you something for drink,
And a matter of money to put in your poke;
But, as for the guilders, what we spoke
Of them, as you very well know, was in joke.
Beside, our losses have made us thrifty.
A thousand guilders! Come, take fifty!"

X

The piper's face fell, and he cried
"No trifling! I can't wait, beside!
I've promised to visit by dinner-time
Bagdat, and accept the prime
Of the Head-Cook's pottage, all he's rich in,
For having left, in the Caliph's kitchen,
Of a nest of scorpions no survivor:
With him I proved no bargain-driver,
With you, don't think I'll bate a stiver!
And folks who put me in a passion
May find me pipe after another fashion."

XI

"How?" cried the Mayor, "d'ye think I brook
Being worse treated than a Cook?
Insulted by a lazy ribald
With idle pipe and vesture piebald?
You threaten us, fellow? Do your worst,
Blow your pipe there till you burst!"

XII

Once more he stept into the street
　And to his lips again
　　Laid his long pipe of smooth straight cane;
And ere he blew three notes (such sweet
Soft notes as yet musician's cunning
　Never gave the enraptured air)
There was a rustling that seemed like a bustling
Of merry crowds justling at pitching and hustling,
Small feet were pattering, wooden shoes clattering,
Little hands clapping and little tongues chattering,
And, like fowls in a farm-yard when barley is scattering,
Out came the children running.
All the little boys and girls,
With rosy cheeks and flaxen curls,
And sparkling eyes and teeth like pearls,
Tripping and skipping, ran merrily after
The wonderful music with shouting and laughter.

XIII

The Mayor was dumb, and the Council stood
As if they were changed into blocks of wood,
Unable to move a step, or cry
To the children merrily skipping by,

—Could only follow with the eye
That joyous crowd at the Piper's back.
But how the Mayor was on the rack,
And the wretched Council's bosoms beat,
As the Piper turned from the High Street
To where the Weser rolled its waters
Right in the way of their sons and daughters!
However he turned from South to West,
And to Koppelberg Hill his steps addressed,
And after him the children pressed;
Great was the joy in every breast.
"He never can cross that mighty top!
He's forced to let the piping drop,
And we shall see our children stop!"
When, lo, as they reached the mountain-side,
A wondrous portal opened wide,
As if a cavern was suddenly hollowed;
And the Piper advanced and the children followed,
And when all were in to the very last,
The door in the mountain-side shut fast.
Did I say all? No! One was lame,
    And could not dance the whole of the way;
And in after years, if you would blame
    His sadness, he was used to say,—
"It's dull in our town since my playmates left!
I can't forget that I'm bereft
Of all the pleasant sights they see,
Which the Piper also promised me.
For he led us, he said, to a joyous land,
Joining the town and just at hand,
Where waters gushed and fruit-trees grew,
And flowers put forth a fairer hue,
And everything was strange and new;

The sparrows were brighter than peacocks here.
And their dogs outran our fallow deer,
And honey-bees had lost their stings,
And horses were born with eagles' wings:
And just as I became assured
My lame foot would be speedily cured,
The music stopped and I stood still,
And found myself outside the hill,
Left alone against my will,
To go now limping as before,
And never hear of that country more!"

XIV

Alas, alas for Hamelin!
   There came into many a burgher's pate
   A text which says, that heaven's gate
   Opes to the rich at as easy rate
As the needle's eye takes a camel in!
The Mayor sent East, West, North, and South,
To offer the Piper, by word of mouth,
   Wherever it was men's lot to find him.
Silver and gold to his heart's content,
If he'd only return the way he went,
   And bring the children behind him.
But when they saw 'twas a lost endeavour,
And Piper and dancers were gone for ever,
They made a decree that lawyers never
   Should think their records dated duly
If, after the day of the month and year,
These words did not as well appear,
"And so long after what happened here
   On the twenty-second of July,
Thirteen hundred and seventy-six":

And the better in memory to fix
The place of the children's last retreat,
They called it, the Pied Piper's Street—
Where any one playing on pipe or tabor
Was sure for the future to lose his labour.
Nor suffered they hostelry or tavern
   To shock with mirth a street so solemn;
But opposite the place of the cavern
   They wrote the story on a column,
And on the great church window painted
The same, to make the world acquainted
How their children were stolen away;
And there it stands to this very day.
And I must not omit to say
That in Transylvania there's a tribe
Of alien people who ascribe
The outlandish ways and dress
On which their neighbours lay such stress,
To their fathers and mothers having risen
Out of some subterraneous prison
Into which they were trepanned
Long time ago in a mighty band
Out of Hamelin town in Brunswick land,
But how or why, they don't understand.

XV

So, Willy, let you and me be wipers
Of scores out with all men—especially pipers:
And, whether they pipe us free fròm rats or fròm mice,
If we've promised them aught, let us keep our promise!
Robert Browning.

˙Lochinvar ∾ ∾ ∾ ∾ ∾

O, YOUNG Lochinvar is come out of the west,
Through all the wide Border his steed was the best;
And save his good broadsword he weapons had none,
He rode all unarm'd, and he rode all alone.
So faithful in love, and so dauntless in war,
That never was knight like the young Lochinvar.

He staid not for brake, and he stopp'd not for stone,
He swam the Eske river where ford there was none;
But ere he alighted at Netherby gate,
The bride had consented, the gallant came late:
For a laggard in love, and a dastard in war,
Was to wed the fair Ellen of brave Lochinvar.

So boldly he enter'd the Netherby Hall,
Among bride's-men, and kinsmen, and brothers, and all:
Then spoke the bride's father, his hand on his sword
(For the poor craven bridegroom said never a word),
"O come ye in peace here, or come ye in war,
Or to dance at our bridal, young Lord Lochinvar?"

"I long woo'd your daughter, my suit you denied;—
Love swells like the Solway, but ebbs like its tide—
And now am I come, with this lost love of mine,
To lead but one measure, drink one cup of wine,
There are maidens in Scotland more lovely by far,
That would gladly be bride to the young Lochinvar."

The bride kiss'd the goblet: the knight took it up,
He quaff'd off the wine, and he threw down the cup,
She look'd down to blush, and she look'd up to sigh,

With a smile on her lips, and a tear in her eye.
He took her soft hand, ere her mother could bar,—
"Now tread we a measure!" said young Lochinvar.

So stately his form, and so lovely her face,
That never a hall such a galliard did grace;
While her mother did fret, and her father did fume,
And the bridegroom stood dangling his bonnet and plume;
And the bride-maidens whisper'd, "'Twere better by far,
To have match'd our fair cousin with young Lochinvar."

One touch of her hand, and one word in her ear,
When they reach'd the hall-door, and the charger stood near;
So light to the croupe the fair lady he swung,
So light to the saddle before her he sprung!
"She is won! we are gone, over bank, bush, and scaur;
They'll have fleet steeds that follow," quoth young Lochinvar.

There was mounting 'mong Graemes of the Netherby clan;
Forsters, Fenwicks, and Musgraves, they rode and they ran:
There was racing and chasing on Cannobie Lee,
But the lost bride of Netherby ne'er did they see.
So daring in love, and so dauntless in war,
Have ye e'er heard of gallant like young Lochinvar?

Sir Walter Scott.

The Mountain and the Squirrel   ◇   ◇

THE mountain and the squirrel
   Had a quarrel,
And the former called the latter " Little prig " ;
Bun replied,
" You are doubtless very big,
But all sorts of things and weather
Must be taken in together
To make up a year,
And a sphere.
And I think it no disgrace
To occupy my place—
If I'm not so large as you,
You are not so small as I,
And not half so spry :
I'll not deny you make
A very pretty squirrel track.
Talents differ ; all is well and wisely put ;
If I cannot carry forests on my back,
Neither can you crack a nut ! "

R. W. Emerson.

BEDTIME

Lady Moon ∽ ∽ ∽

(*How to tell her age.*)

O LADY Moon, your horns point toward the east:
   Shine, be increased;
O Lady Moon, your horns point toward the west:
   Wane, be at rest.

Christina G. Rossetti.

The Star ∽ ∽ ∽

TWINKLE, twinkle, little star,
   How I wonder what you are
Up above the world so high,
Like a diamond in the sky.
Twinkle, twinkle, little star,
How I wonder what you are.

When the blazing sun is gone,
When he nothing shines upon,
Then you show your little light,
Twinkle, twinkle, all the night.
Twinkle, twinkle, little star,
How I wonder what you are.

Then the traveller in the dark
Thanks you for your tiny spark,
He could not see where to go
If you did not twinkle so.
Twinkle, twinkle, little star,
How I wonder what you are.

In the dark blue sky you keep,
While you through·my curtains peep,
And you never shut your eye
Till the sun is in the sky.
Twinkle, twinkle, little star,
How I wonder what you are.

Anon.

The White Paternoster ∽ ∽

MATTHEW, Mark, Luke and John,
    Bless the bed that I lie on !
  Four corners to my bed,
  Five angels there lie spread ;
    Two at my head,
    Two at my feet,
One at my heart, my soul to keep.

Old Rhyme.

Lullaby to an Infant Chief ∽

O, HUSH thee, my babie, thy sire was a knight,
    Thy mother a lady, both lovely and bright ;
The woods and the glens, from the towers which we see,
They all are belonging, dear babie, to thee.
    O ho ro, i ri ri, cadul gu lo.

O, fear not the bugle, though loudly it blows,
It calls but the warders that guard thy repose;
Their bows would be bended, their blades would be red,
Ere the step of a foeman draws near to thy bed.
          O ho ro, i ri ri, cadul gu lo.

O, hush thee, my babie, the time will soon come,
When thy sleep shall be broken by trumpet and drum;
Then hush thee, my darling, take rest while you may,
For strife comes with manhood, and waking with day.
          O ho ro, i ri ri, cadul gu lo.
                                        Sir Walter Scott.

Dutch Lullaby   〰   〰   〰   〰

WYNKEN, Blynken, and Nod one night
      Sailed off in a wooden shoe,—
Sailed on a river of misty light
      Into a sea of dew.
"Where are you going, and what do you wish?"
      The old man asked the three.
"We have come to fish for the herring-fish
      That live in the beautiful sea;
      Nets of silver and gold have we,"
                  Said Wynken,
                  Blynken,
                  And Nod.

The old moon laughed and sung a song
      As they rocked in the wooden shoe;
And the wind that sped them all night long
      Ruffled the waves of dew;
The little stars were the herring-fish

                  x

That lived in that beautiful sea.
"Now cast your nets wherever you wish,
But never afeared are we!"
So cried the stars to the fishermen three,
      Wynken,
      Blynken,
      And Nod.

All night long their nets they threw
  For the fish in the twinkling foam,
Then down from the sky came the wooden shoe,
  Bringing the fishermen home;
'Twas all so pretty a sail, it seemed
  As if it could not be;
And some folk thought 'twas a dream they'd dreamed
  Of sailing that beautiful sea:
But I shall name you the fishermen three:
      Wynken,
      Blynken,
      And Nod.

Wynken and Blynken are two little eyes,
  And Nod is a little head,
And the wooden shoe that sailed the skies
  Is a wee one's trundle-bed;
So shut your eyes while Mother sings
  Of wonderful sights that be,
And you shall see the beautiful things
  As you rock in the misty sea
Where the old shoe rocked the fishermen three,—
      Wynken,
      Blynken,
      And Nod.

Eugene Field.

Queen Mab ❧ ❧ ❧ ❧

A LITTLE fairy comes at night,
 Her eyes are blue, her hair is brown,
With silver spots upon her wings,
 And from the moon she flutters down.

She has a little silver wand,
 And when a good child goes to bed
She waves her hand from right to left,
 And makes a circle round its head.

And then it dreams of pleasant things,
 Of fountains filled with fairy fish,
And trees that bear delicious fruit,
 And bow their branches at a wish:

Of arbours filled with dainty scents
 From lovely flowers that never fade;
Bright flies that glitter in the sun,
 And glow-worms shining in the shade.

And talking birds with gifted tongues,
 For singing songs and telling tales,
And pretty dwarfs to show the way
 Through fairy hills and fairy dales.

But when a bad child goes to bed,
 From left to right she weaves her rings,
And then it dreams all through the night
 Of only ugly horrid things!

Then lions come with glaring eyes,
 And tigers growl, a dreadful noise,
And ogres draw their cruel knives,
 To shed the blood of girls and boys.

Then stormy waves rush on to drown,
  Or raging flames come scorching round,
Fierce dragons hover in the air,
  And serpents crawl along the ground.

Then wicked children wake and weep,
  And wish the long black gloom away;
But good ones love the dark, and find
  The night as pleasant as the day.

                              Thomas Hood.

A Fairy Song   ～   ～   ～

COME, follow, follow me,
  Ye fairy elves that be,
Light tripping o'er the green,
Come follow Mab your queen;
Hand in hand we'll dance around,
For this place is fairy ground.

When mortals are at rest,
And snoring in their nest,
Unheard and unespied,
Through the keyholes we do glide;
Over tables, stools, and shelves,
We trip it with our fairy elves.

And, if the house be foul
With platter, dish, or bowl,
Upstairs we nimbly creep
And find the sluts asleep:
Then we pinch their arms and thighs,
None us hears, nor none espies.

But if the house be swept,
And from uncleanness kept,
We praise the household maid,
And duly she is paid:
Every night before we go
We drop a tester in her shoe.

Then o'er a mushroom's head,
Our tablecloth we spread;
A grain of rye or wheat,
The diet that we eat;
Pearly drops of dew we drink,
In acorn cups filled to the brink.

The brains of nightingales,
With unctuous fat of snails,
Between two cockles stewed,
Is meat that's easy chewed;
Tails of worms and marrow of mice
Do make a dish that's wondrous nice.

The grasshopper, gnat, and fly,
Serve for our minstrelsy,
Grace said, we dance awhile,
And so the time beguile;
And if the moon doth hide her head,
The glow-worm lights us home to bed.

O'er tops of dewy grass
So nimbly do we pass,
The young and tender stalk
Ne'er bends where we do walk;
Yet in the morning may be seen
Where we the night before have been.

Old Song.

The Fairies ∽ ∽

U P the airy mountain,
   Down the rushy glen,
We daren't go a-hunting
   For fear of little men;
Wee folk, good folk,
   Trooping all together:
Green jacket, red cap,
   And white owl's feather!

Down along the rocky shore
   Some make their home,
They live on crispy pancakes
   Of yellow tide-foam;
Some in the reeds
   Of the black mountain-lake,
With frogs for their watch-dogs,
   All night awake.

High on the hill-top
   The old King sits;
He is now so old and gray
   He's nigh lost his wits.
With a bridge of white mist
   Columbkill he crosses,
On his stately journeys
   From Slieveleague to Rosses;
Or going up with music
   On cold starry nights,
To sup with the Queen
   Of the gay Northern Lights.

They stole little Bridget
   For seven years long;

When she came down again
  Her friends were all gone.
They took her lightly back,
  Between the night and morrow,
They thought that she was fast asleep,
  But she was dead with sorrow.
They have kept her ever since
  Deep within the lake,
On a bed of flag-leaves,
  Watching till she wake.

By the craggy hill-side,
  Through the mosses bare,
They have planted thorn-trees
  For pleasure here and there.
Is any man so daring
  As dig them up in spite,
He shall find their sharpest thorns
  In his bed at night.

Up the airy mountain,
  Down the rushy glen,
We daren't go a-hunting
  For fear of little men :
Wee folk, good folk,
  Trooping all together ;
Green jacket, red cap,
  And white owl's feather !

William Allingham.

A FEW
REMARKS

Page 3.   "Happy Thought"   〜

This piece, together with " Windy Nights" (p. 13),
"Whole Duty of Children" (p. 153), and "The Lamplighter"
(p. 205), is from the late Robert Louis Stevenson's book,
A Child's Garden of Verse, *published by Messrs. Longmans*
and Co., *and, with Mr. Robinson's delightful pictures, by*
Mr. John Lane. *The following poem is by Mr. Norman*
Gale, *and is taken from his* Songs for Little People,
published by Messrs. Constable and Co. :—

The Lost Friend

ALL underneath the restless sea
   Grief ran along a wire to me;
Children, your tender friend is gone—
Dear Robert Louis Stevenson.

With radiant smiles he reached his hands
To stroke the young of many lands;
Himself a man and boy in one—
Dear Robert Louis Stevenson.

Since he shall live on children's lips
In tales of treasure and of ships
What need to raise a tower of stone
For Robert Louis Stevenson?

Samoa nurses him in flowers,
For ever hers, for ever ours;
Incarnate tune, undying tone,
Dear Robert Louis Stevenson.

Page 3. "The World's Music" ᘐ ᘐ

This piece is from The Child World, *by Gabriel Setoun, published by Mr. John Lane.* "Jack Frost" (*p. 26*) *is from the same book.*

Page 19. "Pippa's Song" ᘐ ᘐ ᘐ

Pippa was a little Italian, one of the work-girls in a silk mill at Asolo, near Florence. One day she took a long holiday, and passed singing through the white town; and as she sang, certain persons heard her and were never quite the same afterwards. This was one of Pippa's songs. The story of that day is told in a play by Robert Browning, called Pippa Passes, *from which the song is taken.*

Page 19. " The First of May " ◠

May Day is no longer what it was. The following verses,
written in 1825, show what those of us who live in London
now miss :—

Old May Day

IN London, thirty years ago,
  When pretty milkmaids went about,
It was a goodly sight to see
  Their May-Day Pageant all drawn out.

Themselves in comely colours drest,
  Their shining garland in the middle,
A pipe and tabor on before,
  Or else the foot-inspiring fiddle.

They stopt at houses, where it was
  Their custom to cry " Milk below ! "
And while the music play'd, with smiles
  Join'd hands, and pointed toe to toe.

Thus they tripp'd on, till—from the door
  The hop'd-for annual present sent—
A signal came, to curtsey low,
  And at that door cease merriment.

Such scenes and sounds once blest my eyes,
  And charm'd my ears—but all have vanish'd !
On May Day, now, no garlands go,
  For milkmaids, and their dance, are banish'd.

Page 20.   " Child's Song in Spring "   ᵔ

This dainty song is printed in A Pomander of Verse, *by E. Nesbit, published by Mr. John Lane.*

Page 23.   " The Holly "   ᵔ   ᵔ   ᵔ

Mr. Hawker, the author, who was vicar of Morwenstow, in Cornwall, for many years, put this note to the poem :—

" In old simple-hearted Cornwall, the household names 'Uncle' and 'Aunt' were uttered and used as they are to this day in many countries of the East, not only as phrases of kindred, but as words of kindly greeting and tender respect.   It was in the spirit, therefore, of this touching and graphic usage that they were wont on the Tamar side to call the Mother of God in their loyal language Modryb Marya, or Aunt Mary."

Page 27.   " Snow in Town "   ᵔ   ᵔ

Neither of Mr. Rickman Mark's pieces—" Snow in Town" and " The Boy Decides" (p. 207)—which I am enabled to use, has been printed before.

Page 39. "A Song of Saint Francis" ∽

These beautiful lines are from a poetical play called The Husband of Poverty, *by Mr. Henry Neville Maugham, published by Mr. Elliot Stock.*

The Country Life ∽ ∽ ∽ ∽

A very serious fault of this section is the absence of a blacksmith's song. I tried in vain to find one that was good enough. Every poet ought to sing of the glory of the forge. In order that the blacksmith may not be altogether left out, I give a portion of an old ditty that once was sung in villages on St. Clement's Day (23rd November), St. Clement being the blacksmith's patron saint :—

A WORKING smith all other trades excels,
    In useful labour wheresoe'er he dwells ;
Toss up your caps, ye sons of Vulcan, then,
For there are none of all the sons of men
That can with the brave working smiths compare ;
Their work is hard, and jolly lads they are.
What though a smith looks sometimes very black,
And sometimes gets but one shirt to his back,
And that is out at elbows, and so thin
That you through twenty holes may see his skin ;
Yet when he's drest and clean, you all will say,
That smiths are men not made of common clay.

They serve the living, and they serve the dead,
They serve the mitre and the crowned head,
They all are men of honour and renown,
Honest, and just, and loyal to the crown.

Page 48. " The Useful Plough " ∽ ∽

*There are more lines to this fine old song, but the best of it
is given here.   One version of the following ditty is to be
found, with music, in* Songs of the West, *by the Rev. S.
Baring-Gould and the Rev. H. Fleetwood Sheppard, published
by Messrs. Methuen and Co. :—*

The Painful Plough

O ADAM was a ploughboy, when ploughing first began,
The next that did succeed him was Cain, his eldest son.
Some of the generation the calling still pursue,
That bread may not be wanting, they labour at the plough.

Samson was the strongest man, and Solomon was wise,
And Alexander conquering, he made the world his prize,
King David was a valiant man, and many thousands slew ;
Yet none of all these heroes bold could live without the
plough.

Behold the wealthy merchant, that trades on foreign seas,
And brings home gold and treasure for such as live at ease,
With spices and with cinnamon, and oranges also too,
They're brought us from the Indies, by virtue of the plough.

For they must have bread, biscuit, rice-pudding, flour, and
      peas,
To feed the jolly sailors as they sail o'er the seas;
And the man that brings them will own to what is true,
He cannot sail the ocean without the painful plough!

I hope there's none offended at me for singing this,
For never I intended to sing you aught amiss;
And if you will consider, you'll find the saying true,
That all mankind dependeth upon the painful plough.

Page 49. "The Water-Mill" 〜 〜 〜

*This piece, together with "Pussy-Cat" (p. 106) and
"Dame Duck's First Lecture on Education" (p. 111), is
from* Aunt Effie's Rhymes for Little Children, *published in
1858, with illustrations by Hablôt K. Browne ("Phiz").
It is now out of print*

Page 72. "Cherries" 〜 〜 〜 〜

*This piece and that on p. 105, "The Cats' Tea-Party,"
are from* The Illustrated Children's Birthday Book, *edited
by Mr. F. E. Weatherley, and published by Messrs. Myers
and Co. The following little song, sung by fairies robbing
an orchard, shows that birds are not the only "boys for
fruit" :—*

Y

WE the Fairies, blithe and antic,
    Of dimensions not gigantic,
Though the moonshine mostly keep us,
Oft in orchards frisk and peep us.

Stolen sweets are always sweeter,
Stolen kisses much completer,
Stolen looks are nice in chapels,
Stolen, stolen be your apples.

When to bed the world are bobbing,
Then's the time for orchard-robbing;
Yet the fruit were scarce worth peeling
Were it not for stealing, stealing.

Leigh Hunt (from the Italian).

Page 73. " The Cuckoo's Voice "   ⌒

A writer in St. Nicholas *explains why the cuckoo says only its own name from morning to night :—*

ONCE from the town a starling flew,
    And on the road there met his view
A cuckoo, who to him did say :
"What is the news from town to-day?"
Said he : "The nightingale's sweet lays
Receive from all the greatest praise.
The thrush, the blackbird, and the wren,
Are slightly mentioned now and then."
Then said the cuckoo anxiously :

"Pray tell me what they say of me."
The starling faltered, then replied,
What greatly hurt the cuckoo's pride:
"That is a thing I cannot do,
Because none ever speak of you."
The cuckoo tossing, then, his head,
In anger to the starling said:
"I'll be revenged, and will from spite
Sing of myself from morn till night."

Page 75.   "Eagles"   ❧   ❧   ❧   ❧

The complete piece, of which these lines are a portion, is to be found in the late Jean Ingelow's Poems, *published by Messrs. Longmans and Co.*

Page 76.   "The Burial of the Linnet"   ❧

From the late Mrs. Ewing's Papa Poodle and other Pets, *published by the S.P.C.K.   It is also in* Songs for Music, *by Four Friends, published by Messrs. King and Co.*

Page 87.   "The Ballad of Jenny the Mare"   ❧

From Euphranor, *by Edward Fitzgerald.*

Page 91.   " Epitaph on a Hare "   ◡

In one of his letters, written on 21st August 1780, Cowper
tells how Puss, his other hare, of which he speaks in the last
two stanzas, ran away and was brought back again.   This is
the story :—

" Last Wednesday night, while we were at supper, between
the hours of eight and nine, I heard an unusual noise in the
back parlour, as if one of the hares was entangled, and
endeavouring to disengage herself.   I was just going to rise
from the table, when it ceased.   In about five minutes, a
voice on the outside of the parlour door inquired if one of
my hares had got away.   I immediately rushed into the next
room, and found that my poor favourite Puss had made her
escape.   She had gnawed in sunder the strings of a lattice-
work, with which I thought I had sufficiently secured the
window, and which I preferred to any other sort of blind,
because it admitted plenty of air.   From thence I hastened
to the kitchen, where I saw the redoubtable Thomas Free-
man, who told me, that having seen her, just after she had
dropped into the street, he attempted to cover her with his
hat, but she screamed out, and leaped directly over his head.
I then desired him to pursue as fast as possible, and added
Richard Coleman to the chase, as being nimbler, and carry-
ing less weight than Thomas ; not expecting to see her again,
but desirous to learn, if possible, what became of her.   In
something less than an hour, Richard returned, almost
breathless, with the following account.   That soon after he
began to run, he left Tom behind him and came in sight of
a most numerous hunt of men, women, children, and dogs ;
that he did his best to keep back the dogs, and presently
outstripped the crowd, so that the race was at last disputed

between himself and Puss;—she ran right through the town, and down the lane that leads to Dropshort; a little before she came to the house, he got the start and turned her; she pushed for the town again, and soon after she entered it, sought shelter in Mr. Wagstaff's tan-yard, adjoining to old Mr. Drake's. Sturge's harvest-men were at supper, and saw her from the opposite side of the way. There she encountered the tan-pits full of water; and while she was struggling out of one pit and plunging into another, and almost drowned, one of the men drew her out by the ears and secured her. She was then well washed in a bucket, to get the lime out of her coat, and brought home in a sack at ten o'clock.

This frolic cost us four shillings, but you may believe we did not grudge a farthing of it. The poor creature received only a little hurt in one of her claws, and in one of her ears, and is now almost as well as ever."

Page 97. "Birds, Beasts, and Fishes" ᔆ ᔆ

This piece, together with all those signed Ann and Jane Taylor, is from the Original Poems, *by the two sisters whose verses for children have been more widely read and remembered than those of any writer. I have put both names to every extract, for although not all of them were written jointly, the sisters must always have considered them together. The* Original Poems *were published first in 1805, and since then there have been very many editions. A selection, illustrated by Miss Kate Greenaway, came out in 1883, under the title* Little Ann and Her Mother. *Ann Taylor, who was born in 1782, afterwards became Mrs. Gilbert, and lived until 1866; Jane died unmarried in 1824, at the age of forty-one. She began to rhyme quite early. When only eight she asked her father for a garden of her own in the following manner :—*

A H, dear papa, did you but know
    The trouble of your Jane,
I'm sure you would relieve me now,
    And ease me of my pain.

Although your garden is but small,
    And more, indeed, you crave,
There's one small bit not used at all,
    And this I wish to have.

A pretty garden I would make
    That you would like to know ;
Then pray, papa, for pity's sake
    This bit of ground bestow.

Page 110. " The Three Little Pigs " ～　　～

In Aunt Judy's Song Book, *from which this piece is taken, it has a musical setting by Mr. Scott-Gatty. " The Burial of the Linnet " (p. 76), in the same work, is also arranged as a song.*

Page 123. " Jemima " ～　～　～　～

Some people prefer the following version of the same piece. The other seems to me to be better. It was surely much finer

for Jemima to hurrah with her heels than to drum them against
the winder, which any one could do :—

THERE was a little girl, who had a little curl
    Right in the middle of her forehead,
And when she was good she was very, very good,
    But when she was bad she was horrid.

She stood on her head, on her little truckle-bed,
    With nobody by for to hinder ;
She screamed and she squalled, she yelled and she bawled,
    And drummed her little heels against the winder.

Her mother heard the noise, and thought it was the boys
    Playing in the empty attic,
She rushed upstairs, and caught her unawares,
    And spanked her, most emphatic.

I have tried in vain to discover the author of these verses.
According to an American writer, Miss Roosevelt, the first
stanza was claimed by Longfellow ; but there is no proof that
it was he who finished it.

Page 123. " A Strange Wild Song " ᔕ ᔕ

This is the Song of the Gardener in Sylvie and Bruno, *by*
Lewis Carroll, published by Messrs. Macmillan and Co. " *The*
Walrus and the Carpenter" (*p. 130*), *it is unnecessary to state,*
is from the same author's Through the Looking-Glass.

Page 125.   " Sage Counsel "   ∽   ∽   ∽

*Mr. A. T. Quiller Couch has kindly given me leave to use
these verses, which have not been published before.*

Page 126.   " The Elephant "   ∽   ∽   ∽

*"The Elephant" and "The Lion" (p. 126), "The Frog"
and "The Ode to a Rhinoceros" (p. 127), are from* The
Bad Child's Book of Beasts, *the Introduction to which is
printed on p. 155.* The Bad Child's Book of Beasts *was
written by H. B., and illustrated by B. T. B., and is
published by Messrs. Alden of Oxford. The verses and
pictures go so perfectly together that it is almost a pity to
divide them : I hope that these extracts may send readers to
the book.*

Page 127.   " The Frog "   ∽   ∽   ∽

*Another writer, Mr. Ashby Sterry, has gone farther than
the author of "The Frog" as a friend of dumb creatures.
Here are two stanzas from a warm-hearted appeal which he
once made in* Punch :—

SPEAK gently to the herring, and kindly to the calf,
   Be blithesome with the bunny, at barnacles don't laugh !
Give nuts unto the monkey, and buns unto the bear,
Ne'er hint at currant jelly if you chance to see a hare !

O, little girls, pray hide your combs when tortoises draw
    nigh,
And never in the hearing of a pigeon whisper Pie!
But give the stranded jelly-fish a shove into the sea—
Be always kind to animals wherever you may be!

O, make not game of sparrows, nor faces at the ram,
And ne'er allude to mint sauce when calling on a lamb,
Don't beard the thoughtful oyster, don't dare the cod to
    crimp,
Don't cheat the pike or ever try to pot the playful shrimp.
Tread lightly on the turning worm, don't bruise the butterfly,
Don't ridicule the wry-neck, nor sneer at salmon-fry;
O, ne'er delight to make dogs fight, nor bantams disagree—
Be always kind to animals wherever you may be!

Page 134. "The Pobble Who Has No Toes"

I should like also to have printed other of Edward Lear's
Nonsense Songs, *published by Messrs. Warne and Co., but
copyright prevented. By those who know that volume, and
also* The Book of Nonsense *and* More Nonsense, *the following examination paper, which was drawn up some years ago
by Mr. C. L. Graves, and printed in the* Spectator, *should be
worth attempting:—*

1. What do you gather from a study of Mr. Lear's works
to have been the prevalent characteristics of the inhabitants
of Gretna, Prague, Thermopylæ, Wick, and Hong-Kong?
2. State briefly what historical events are connected with
Ischia, Chertsey, Whitehaven, Boulak, and Jellibolee.

3. Comment, with illustrations, upon Mr. Lear's use of the following words :—Runcible, propitious, dolomphious, borascible, fizzgiggious, himmeltanious, tumble-dum-down, spongetaneous.

4. Enumerate accurately all the animals who lived on the Quangle Wangle's Hat, and explain how the Quangle Wangle was enabled at once to enlighten his five travelling companions as to the true nature of the Co-operative Cauliflower.

5. What were the names of the five daughters of the Old Person of China, and what was the purpose for which the Old Man of the Dargle purchased six barrels of Gargle?

6. Collect notices of King Xerxes in Mr. Lear's works, and state your theory, if you have any, as to the character and appearance of Nupiter Piffkin.

7. Draw pictures of the Plum-pudding Flea and the Moppsikon Floppsikon Bear, and state by whom waterproof tubs were first used.

Page 137. "The Story of Little Suck-a-Thumb"

I have borrowed this piece from Struwwelpeter *because I wanted to include something of Dr. Hoffmann's in this book; but it is, of course, a little unfair to separate the verse from the pictures. The following lines are taken from an ode in memory of Dr. Hoffmann which appeared in the* Spectator *soon after his death in 1894 :—*

THY pencil, too,—with what a force
   It shadowed Nemesis, her course !
Who that once saw, can e'er forget,
The cats which mourned for Harriet,

With eyes so grievously attacked
By all the pains of cataract?
Or Peter's own despondent form?
Or Robert's very local storm?
Or who without a thrill can scan
The awful "red-legged scissor-man"?

Thy Peter was a beacon-light
To guide my erring steps aright;
For what deters me from the fun
Of mocking Afric's ebon son,
(A kind of sport to which my mind
Is naturally much inclined),
But recollection of the ill
Befalling Arthur, Ned, and Will?
Did not Augustus pine and droop
Through his antipathy to soup,
A cross like his would surely mark
The spot where I lay stiff and stark;
And were it not that cruel Fred
Consumed unpleasant drugs in bed,
I should, I feel it, every day
Defy the R.S.P.C.A.

This wish for thee, then, Mentor rare
Of little people everywhere:
May the earth lightly on thee lie,
May *Struwwelpeter* never die!

Page 139. "The Man in the Moon" ∽ ∽

The Raggedy Man, who tells this story, was what in England is called an odd or handy man. The following description of him is from another of Mr. Riley's poems, written in what is known in America as the Hoosier dialect. A little study will make the words plain:—

O! the Raggedy Man! He works fer Pa;
  An' he's the goodest man ever you saw!
He comes to our house every day,
An' waters the horses, and feeds 'em hay;
An' he opens the shed—an' we all 'ist laugh
When he drives out our little old wobble-ly calf;
An' nen—ef our hired girl says he can—
He milks the cow fer 'Lizabuth Ann.
      Ain't he a awful good Raggedy Man?
          Raggedy! Raggedy! Raggedy Man!

W'y, the Raggedy Man—he's 'ist so good
He splits the kindlin' and chops the wood;
An' nen he spades in our garden, too,
An' does most things 'at boys can't do.
He climbed clean up in our big tree
An' shooked a apple down fer me—
An' nother'n, too, fer 'Lizabuth Ann—
An' nother'n, too, fer the Raggedy Man.
      Ain't he a awful kind Raggedy Man?
          Raggedy! Raggedy! Raggedy Man!

Page 144. " The Wreck of the Steamship *Puffin* "

This is from Mr. Punch's Young Reciter, *by Mr. Anstey,
published by Messrs. Bradbury, Agnew, and Co.   It ought
to be stated that in the book the ballad is accompanied by
directions telling how it ought (or ought not) to be recited.*

Page 153. "Symon's Lesson of Wisdom for all
Manner of Children "   ❧   ❧   ❧   ❧

*The piece from which these lines are taken is four hundred
years old.   By the advice of Dr. Furnivall the spelling has
been made modern ; otherwise everything is as the quaint and
very thorough instructor wrote it.   The Lesson in full is to
be seen in Dr. Furnivall's* Babees' Book, *one of the Early
English Text Society's publications.   Another piece in the
same collection, " The Birched Schoolboy," dated 1500, ends
with the following wish :—*

I WOULD my master were a wat [a hare],
    And my book a wild cat,
And a brace of greyhounds in his top :
I would be glad for to see that !
    What availeth me though I say nay ?

I would my master were a hare,
And all his books hounds were,
And I myself a jolly hunter :
To blow my horn I would not spare !
For if he were dead I would not care.
    What availeth me though I say nay ?

Birching or whipping now grows less and less common. Once it seems to have been continuous. In a school-book published in 1664, I find these threatening verses addressed by the schoolmaster to his pupils :—

M Y child and schollar, take good heed
    Unto the words that here are set,
And see thou do accordingly,
    Or else be sure thou shalt be beat.

First, I command thee God to serve,
    Then to thy Parents duty yield,
Unto all Men be courteous,
    And mannerly in town and field.

If broken Hos'd or Shoo'd you go,
    Or Slovenly in your array,
Without a Girdle or Untrust,
    Then you and I must have a fray.

If that thou cry or talk aloud,
    Or Books do rend, or strike with Knife,
Or Laugh or Play Unlawfully,
    Then you and I must be at strife.

If that you Curse, Miscall, or Swear,
    If that you Pick, Filch, Steal, or Lye,
If you forget a Schollar's part,
    Then must you sure your points untye.

Wherefore, my child, behave thy self
  So decently in all thy ways
That thou may'st purchase Parents' love,
  And eke obtain thy Master's praise.

*Counsel (the title of this section) usually means counsel
from the old to the young, but there is also counsel upside-
down, as we might call it. In St. Nicholas is the following
example, called "A Lesson for Mamma," by Sydney Dayre :—*

DEAR mother, if you just could be
  A tiny little girl like me,
And I your mother, you would see
  How nice I'd be to you.
I'd always let you have your way ;
I'd never frown at you and say :
"You are behaving ill to-day ;
  Such conduct will not do."

I'd always give you jelly-cake
For breakfast, and I'd never shake
My head, and say : "You must not take
  So very large a slice."
I'd never say : "My dear, I trust
You will not make me say you *must*
Eat up your oatmeal"; or, "The crust
  You'll find is very nice."

I'd buy you candy every day ;
I'd go down town with you, and say :
"What would my darling like? You may
  Have anything you see."

I'd never say: "My pet, you know
'Tis bad for health and teeth, and so
I cannot let you have it.   No;
    It would be wrong in me."

And every day I'd let you wear
Your nicest dress, and never care
If it should get a great big tear;
    I'd only say to you:
"My precious treasure, never mind,
For little clothes *will* tear, I find."
Now, mother, wouldn't that be kind?
    That's just what *I* should do.

I'd never say: "Well, just *a few!*"
I'd let you stop your lessons, too;
I'd say: "They are too hard for you,
    Poor child, to understand."
I'd put the books and slates away;
You shouldn't do a thing but play,
And have a party every day.
    Ah-h-h! wouldn't that be grand!

But, mother dear, you cannot grow
Into a little girl, you know,
And I can't be your mother; so
    The only thing to do,
Is just for you to try and see
How very, very nice 'twould be
For *you* to do all this for *me*.
    Now, mother, *couldn't* you?

Page 156. "How to Look when Speaking"   ∽

All the pieces signed, like this, with the name of Elizabeth Turner, are taken from little books of "Cautionary Stories" for children, which were published in the first twenty years of this century. One was The Daisy, one The Cowslip, one The Crocus. *For long they were favourites in the nursery, and as recently as 1885* The Daisy *was reprinted by Messrs. Griffith and Farran. Mrs. Elizabeth Turner, who lived at Whitechurch in Shropshire, died in 1846.*

Marjorie Fleming, Poetess   ∽   ∽   ∽   ∽

Marjorie Fleming, who wrote these pieces, was a little Scotch girl, a friend of Sir Walter Scott. She was born on 15th January 1803, and died the 19th December 1811, before she was quite nine. You will find an account of her life in a book by Dr. John Brown, called John Leech and Other Papers (*published by Messrs. A. and C. Black*). *Marjorie Fleming was one of the world's most delightful children.*

Page 181. "Going into Breeches" ∽   ∽   ∽

This piece, together with "Feigned Courage," on p. 184, and "Choosing a Profession," on p. 339, is from Poetry for Children, *a little book, published in 1809, which was written*

z

by Mary Lamb and her brother Charles. Writing to Coleridge, the poet, in 1809, Charles Lamb says, "Perhaps you will admire the number of subjects, all of children, picked out by an old bachelor and an old maid. Many parents would not have found so many." Mary Lamb wrote the greater part of the book, and I have therefore put her name to these pieces.

Page 195. "The Two Gardens" ❧ ❧ ❧

These verses give an opportunity of printing another piece that bears upon the junior garden—I mean the garden in the corner of the garden. It is in Mr. Norman Gale's Songs for Little People :—

Mustard and Cress

ELIZABETH, my cousin, is the sweetest little girl,
    From her eyes like dark blue pansies, to her tiniest
        golden curl ;
I do not use her great long name, but simply call her Bess,
And yesterday I planted her in mustard and in cress.

My garden is so narrow that there's very little room,
But I'd rather have her name than get a hollyhock to bloom ;
And before she comes to visit us with Charley and with
        Jess,
She'll pop up green and bonny out of mustard and of cress.

Looking Forward ᴖ ᴖ ᴖ ᴖ ᴖ

This section is very incomplete ; but I cannot find other suitable verses dealing with it. One of Mary Lamb's quaint pieces, called " Choosing a Profession," touches the subject :—

A CREOLE boy from the West Indies brought,
　　To be in European learning taught,
Some years before to Westminster he went,
To a preparatory school was sent.
When from his artless tale the mistress found,
The child had not one friend on English ground,
She, even as if she his own mother were,
Made the dark Indian her peculiar care.
Oft on her favourite's future lot she thought ;
To know the bent of his young mind she sought,
For much the kind preceptress wished to find
To what profession he was most inclined,
That where his genius led they might him train ;
For nature's kindly bent she held not vain.
But vain her efforts to explore his will ;
The frequent question he evaded still :
Till on a day at length he to her came,
Joy sparkling in his eyes ; and said, the same
Trade he would be those boys of colour were,
Who danced so happy in the open air.
It was a troop of chimney-sweeping boys,
With wooden music and obstreperous noise,
In tarnished finery and grotesque array,
Were dancing in the street the first of May.

The West Indian's choice was even more difficult to believe in then than it would be now, for that was the time when chimney-sweepers had actually to climb up the chimneys (like Tom in The Water-Babies) *even though the fire was burning. William Blake's " Chimney-Sweeper," from* The Songs of Innocence, *was written when the state of the boys was at its worst:—*

WHEN my mother died I was very young,
  And my father sold me while yet my tongue
Could scarcely cry, "'Weep, 'weep, 'weep, 'weep !"
So your chimneys I sweep and in soot I sleep.

There's little Tom Dacre, who cried when his head,
That curl'd like a lamb's back, was shaved, so I said,
" Hush, Tom, never mind it, for when your head's bare,
You know that the soot cannot spoil your white hair."

And so he was quiet, and that very night,
As Tom was a-sleeping, he had such a sight:
That thousands of sweepers, Dick, Joe, Ned, and Jack,
Were all of them locked up in coffins of black,

And by came an angel who had a bright key,
And he open'd the coffins and set them all free;
Then down a green plain, leaping, laughing, they run,
And wash in a river and shine in the sun.

Then naked and white, all their bags left behind,
They rise upon clouds and sport in the wind;
And the angel told Tom if he'd be a good boy,
He'd have God for his father and never want joy.

And so Tom awoke ; and we rose in the dark,
And got with our bags and our brushes to work.
Though the morning was cold, Tom was happy and warm,
So if all do their duty they need not fear harm.

Page 205. " The Pedlar's Caravan"   ‿   ‿

*This piece, and the " Shooting Song " on the page next it,
are from* The Lilliput Levee, *by Matthew Browne (William
Brighty Rands), which is now out of print.   An illustrated
edition, under the title* Lilliput Lyrics, *may be expected next
year.*

Page 207. " The Boy Decides "   ‿   ‿   ‿

*I have no Looking Forward verses from the point of view
of the little girl, except the following scrap, from a piece by
Miss Laurens Alma-Tadema, printed in her book of poems
entitled* Realms of Unknown Kings, *which is published by
Mr. Grant Richards :—*

IF no one ever marries me
   I shan't mind very much ;
I shall buy a squirrel in a cage
   And a little rabbit-hutch :

I shall have a cottage near a wood,
   And a pony all my own,
And a little lamb quite clean and tame
   That I can take to town :

And when I'm getting really old,
   —At twenty-eight or nine—
I shall buy a little orphan-girl
   And bring her up as mine.

Good Fellows ⌒ ⌒ ⌒ ⌒ ⌒

   *The following piece would be said by those who have
profited by him to belong also to this section :—*

Mr. Nobody

I KNOW a funny little man,
   As quiet as a mouse,
Who does the mischief that is done
   In everybody's house !
There's no one ever sees his face,
   And yet we all agree
That every plate we break was cracked
   By Mr. Nobody.

'Tis he who always tears our books,
   Who leaves the door ajar,
He pulls the buttons from our shirts,
   And scatters pins afar ;
That squeaking door will always squeak
   For, prithee, don't you see,
We leave the oiling to be done
   By Mr. Nobody.

He puts damp wood upon the fire,
  That kettles cannot boil ;
His are the feet that bring in mud,
  And all the carpets soil.
The papers always are mislaid,
  Who had them last but he ?
There's no one tosses them about
  But Mr. Nobody.

The finger-marks upon the door
  By none of us are made ;
We never leave the blinds unclosed,
  To let the curtains fade.
The ink we never spill, the boots
  That lying round you see
Are not our boots ; they all belong
  To Mr. Nobody.

Anon.

Page 228. " The Old Courtier " 〜

The second part of this song deals with the Old Courtier's
Son. It has been judged too melancholy for inclusion here.

Page 243. " The Captain stood on the Carronade "

From Snarleyyow.

Page 251. "The Babes in the Wood" ∾

Here is an old pocket version of the same story:—

M^Y dear, do you know
    How a long time ago,
Two poor little children,
Whose names I don't know,
Were stolen away
On a fine summer's day,
    And left in a wood,
As I've heard people say.

And when it was night,
So sad was their plight,
    The sun it went down
And the moon gave no light!
They sobb'd and they sigh'd,
And they bitterly cried,
    And the poor little things,
They laid down and died.

And when they were dead,
The robins so red
    Brought strawberry leaves.
And over them spread;
And all the day long,
They sang them this song—
Poor babes in the wood!
Poor babes in the wood!
    And don't you remember
The babes in the wood?

Page 303.   "Lady Moon"   ◡   ◡   ◡

From Sing-Song, *by the late Christina G. Rossetti, published by Messrs. Macmillan and Co.*

Page 305.   "Dutch Lullaby"   ◡   ◡

From the late Eugene Field's Little Book of Western Verse, *published by Messrs. Osgood, McIlvaine and Co. There are one or two other pieces by Mr. Field which I should have used had I permission.   You will find them in the book named, and in the* Second Book of Western Verse.

Page 310.   "The Fairies"   ◡   ◡

The late William Allingham's Complete Poetical Works are published by Messrs. Reeves and Turner.   An illustrated edition of " The Fairies" has been published by Messrs. De La Rue and Co.

INDEX OF AUTHORS

POST-SCRIPT

FOR kindly permitting me the use of certain copyright pieces I wish to thank Mrs. Allingham, Miss L. Alma-Tadema, Mr. Arlo Bates, Mr. Hilaire Belloc, Lord Basil Blackwood, "Lewis Carroll," Mr. A. T. Quiller Couch, Mrs. Eden, Dr. Furnivall, Mr. Norman Gale, Mr. C. L. Graves, Mr. Anstey Guthrie, Mr. H. Neville Maugham, "E. Nesbit," Mr. A. S. Scott-Gatty, "Gabriel Setoun," Mr. F. E. Weatherley, and the executors of the late R. L. Stevenson; also the editor of the Boy's Own Paper, the editor of St. Nicholas, the editor of The Spectator, and Messrs. A. and C. Black, Messrs. Bradbury, Agnew, and Co., Mr. John Lane, Messrs. Longmans and Co., Messrs. Macmillan and Co., Messrs. Nister and Co., Messrs. Harper and Brothers, and Messrs. Warne and Co. Certain collections I have found very useful, notably Chappell's Music of the Olden Time, Mr. Ditchfield's Old English Customs, Hullah's Song Book, and Mr. Baring-Gould's Songs of the West. I am also grateful to many friends for advice, and assistance in copying.

E. V. L.

September 1897.